Advance praise for *The Mast*

"This very practical handbook had me completely rethinking how my classes could be structured for a competency-based approach to student achievement. The section about reducing the grading you take home makes so much sense. This book should be read by all educators interesting in engaging students with active and deep learning."

—Meg Ormiston, author, teacher, and educational consultant

"For teachers exploring mastery learning on their own or for schools launching a mastery pilot, Bergmann's book is an invaluable guide into what a mastery classroom can really look like. You'll find everything from lesson plans and classroom arrangements to rubrics and gradebooks, with Bergmann offering his own concrete examples and additional insight from other teachers who are deeply invested in competency-based approaches to teaching and learning."

—Justin Reich, Mitsui Career Development Professor, MIT Comparative Media Studies/Writing and Director, MIT Teaching Systems Lab

"This book is like having a mentor at your side as you plan for mastery learning. It nudges, supports, and guides you as you focus on the biggest of challenges of teaching: making sure every student has mastered the concepts before moving on. An important resource for all teachers."

—Jeane Schocroft, deputy principal, Open Access College, Marden, Australia

"Jonathan Bergmann has provided educators and school leaders with the definitive guide to effectively implement mastery learning in schools. Not only does this book build the case for mastery learning in theory, but it also lays out detailed strategies and proven practices that teachers can readily deploy in their classrooms. If your goal is to learn how mastery and competency-based instruction can fundamentally transform your classroom practice, start here!"

—Tom Driscoll, CEO, EdTechTeacher

"*The Mastery Learning Handbook* is an inspiring, well-thought-out, research-based yet completely practical guide forged in the fire of real-world experiences. It's great not only for educators new to mastery and flipped learning but also for experienced mastery practitioners looking to incorporate the latest research, gain practical tools for troubleshooting, and learning from inspiring stories and tips from teachers around the world."

—Joseph Liaw, instructional innovation coach and physics teacher, Hinsdale Central High School, Hinsdale, Illinois

"An insightful guide for teachers working to understand not just the *why* of mastery learning but also the very practical, day-to-day *how*. Jon Bergmann's research, interviews, first-hand experience, and humility combine to make *The Mastery Learning Handbook* comprehensive, usable, and delightful to read."

—Patricia C. Russell, Chief Learning Officer, Mastery Transcript Consortium

"In this easy-to-read implementation guide, Jon Bergmann identifies the challenges that one is likely to face when implementing mastery learning and explains how he and others have successfully navigated around and through those challenges. He makes the claim, 'This book is going to push you,' and he provides the evidence as to why this kind of push is necessary and leads to greater student engagement and understanding and positive academic outcomes. This book is a must-read for every forward-thinking, future-focused teacher and school administrator."

—*Charles Khoury, superintendent and CEO, Ulster BOCES, Port Ewen, New York*

"If you want to reach your students, if you want to succeed as a teacher, jump into this book: Learn from it and implement its mastery learning cycle. You will not regret it. Jon Bergmann has collected the experience from creative and successful teachers from all over the world, opening up for you the process of mastery learning in an easily understandable format. My advice to all educators: Try it; you will not regret it."

—*Hjalmar Arnason, managing director of Keilir Academy, Reykjanesbaer, Iceland*

"How do educators put mastery learning components together to truly reach each learner? Jonathan Bergmann's guidebook explains in detail and with many examples the steps it will take to revolutionize education with mastery learning. It's time for equitable learning that works for ALL learners!"

—*Maureen O'Shaughnessy, author,* Education Evolution *podcast host, and founding leader of the LEADPrep microschool*

"This book really is about mastery learning done right. Proceeding from Benjamin Bloom's research, author Jonathan Bergmann shows how modern technology brings about possibilities that Bloom could only dream of. Mastery learning has components to support student-owned learning, success for all students, collaborative learning, student metacognition, and deeper learning models such as PBL and authentic learning. This is a great manual for individual educators or a professional learning community book study."

—*Michael Gorman, education consultant and creator of the* 21st Century Educational Technology and Learning *blog*

"Mastery learning has long been an unrealized dream of education giants, who recognized it as a better way to lift outcomes for every student. Thanks to *The Mastery Learning Handbook*, you can now bring that dream to life in your classroom."

—*John Baker, founder and CEO, D2L*

"*The Mastery Learning Handbook* is a necessary and powerful text for teachers working in post–COVID-19 hybrid times—a time when we must rethink the way we teach, the strategies we use, and whether or not we are taking into account the needs of our increasingly diverse students. Jon Bergmann provides guidance and inspiration through his enthusiasm for the mastery learning approach and his love for teaching."

—*Miguel Sedoff, Minister of Education, Science, and Technology, Misiones, Argentina*

The Mastery Learning Handbook

JONATHAN BERGMANN

The Mastery Learning Handbook

A COMPETENCY-BASED APPROACH TO STUDENT ACHIEVEMENT

Arlington, Virginia USA

2800 Shirlington Road, Suite 1001 • Arlington, VA 22206 USA
Phone: 800-933-2723 or 703-578-9600 • Fax: 703-575-5400
Website: www.ascd.org • Email: member@ascd.org
Author guidelines: www.ascd.org/write

Penny Reinart, *Chief Impact Officer;* Genny Ostertag, *Managing Director, Book Acquisitions & Editing;* Allison Scott, *Acquisitions Editor;* Mary Beth Nielsen, *Interim Director, Book Editing;* Katie Martin, *Editor;* Thomas Lytle, *Creative Director;* Donald Ely, *Art Director;* Lisa Hill, *Graphic Designer;* Valerie Younkin, *Senior Production Designer;* Kelly Marshall, *Production Manager;* Shajuan Martin, *E-Publishing Specialist*

Copyright © 2023 Jonathan Bergmann. All rights reserved. By purchasing only authorized electronic or print editions and not participating in or encouraging piracy of copyrighted materials, you support the rights of authors and publishers. Readers may duplicate the reproducible templates linked to in this book for non-commercial use within their school. All other requests to reproduce or republish excerpts of this work in print or electronic format may include a small fee. Please contact the Copyright Clearance Center (CCC), 222 Rosewood Dr., Danvers, MA 01923, USA (phone: 978-750-8400; fax: 978-646-8600; web: www.copyright.com). To inquire about site licensing options or any other reuse, contact ASCD Permissions at www.ascd.org/permissions or permission@ascd.org. For a list of vendors authorized to license ASCD e-books to institutions, see www.ascd.org/epubs. Send translation inquiries to translations@ascd.org.

ASCD® is a registered trademark of Association for Supervision and Curriculum Development. All other trademarks contained in this book are the property of, and reserved by, their respective owners, and are used for editorial and informational purposes only. No such use should be construed to imply sponsorship or endorsement of the book by the respective owners.

All web links in this book are correct as of the publication date below but may have become inactive or otherwise modified since that time. If you notice a deactivated or changed link, please email books@ascd.org with the words "Link Update" in the subject line. In your message, please specify the web link, the book title, and the page number on which the link appears.

PAPERBACK ISBN: 978-1-4166-3142-2   ASCD product #122038   n10/22

PDF EBOOK ISBN: 978-1-4166-3143-9; see Books in Print for other formats.

Quantity discounts are available: email programteam@ascd.org or call 800-933-2723, ext. 5773, or 703-575-5773. For desk copies, go to www.ascd.org/deskcopy.

Library of Congress Cataloging-in-Publication Data
Names: Bergmann, Jonathan, author.
Title: The mastery learning handbook : a competency-based approach to student achievement / Jonathan Bergmann.
Description: Arlington, Virginia : ASCD, 2023. | Includes bibliographical references and index.
Identifiers: LCCN 2022022249 (print) | LCCN 2022022250 (ebook) | ISBN 9781416631422 (paperback) | ISBN 9781416631439 (pdf)
Subjects: LCSH: Competency-based education—United States. | Academic achievement—United States.
Classification: LCC LC1032 .B457 2023 (print) | LCC LC1032 (ebook) | DDC 370.11—dc23/eng/20220707
LC record available at https://lccn.loc.gov/2022022249
LC ebook record available at https://lccn.loc.gov/2022022250

32 31 30 29 28 27 26 25 24 23   1 2 3 4 5 6 7 8 9 10 11 12

The Mastery Learning Handbook

Introduction 1

Part 1: First Things First

    1. The Promise of Mastery Learning 7
    2. Setting the Stage for Mastery Learning 19
    3. Creating Mastery Spaces 25

Part 2: Planning for Mastery Learning

    4. Big Picture Planning 35
    5. Developing Clear Objectives and the Mastery Rubric 38
    6. Planning Your Mastery Assessments 47
    7. Creating Tools for Formative Assessment 56
    8. Creating Independent-Space Learning Objects 62
    9. Creating Group-Space Learning Objects 79
    10. Creating Reflection Opportunities 83
    11. Assessing Mastery 86
    12. Providing Remediation and Feedback 92

Part 3: Mastery Learning in Practice

    13. What Everyday Mastery Learning Looks Like 105
    14. Managing Students Who Master Quickly 108
    15. Grading for Mastery 116
    16. How to Stick with Mastery Learning and Not Give Up 129

Conclusion 145

References 149

Index 151

About the Author 155

Introduction

Imagine that new students come into your classroom almost every week. Many of them haven't been in school for months. They come to you with different skills, different backgrounds, and different levels of parental support. Some come knowing your content. Some come with huge gaps in their knowledge. And some come burdened with pressure from their parents, pressure from themselves, and untold pain.

But wait, you say. *I don't have to imagine. This is my reality.* This was likely the reality for any teacher resuming in-person instruction during the COVID-19 pandemic. Having so many students in so many different places in their learning made for an almost untenable teaching environment.

Corey Sullivan and Tim Kelly certainly don't have to imagine this scenario, either. They teach at a U.S. Department of Defense school in Germany, which regularly takes in new students—many of whom have been out of school for the four to six weeks that the military transfer process often takes. Corey and Tim teach math, a subject that builds on previous knowledge, so this situation makes teaching quite challenging for them.

But Corey's and Tim's students don't miss a beat. Although they arrive in the classroom at different points in their content comprehension, they slide right into where they need to be. The reason is simple: Corey and Tim teach using *mastery learning*. This means they realize that their role is to take students from where they are to the next level. They don't panic when a new student arrives, because their instruction is designed to enable students to move forward at their own pace as they master knowledge, skills, and dispositions. And the results speak for themselves, with Corey's and Tim's students scoring well above their peers on the district's standardized tests.

My Journey to Mastery Learning

My own experience with mastery learning started after my initial foray into the world of flipped learning. I was a career chemistry teacher who, along with Aaron

Sams, was at the forefront of the flipped learning movement. Aaron and I have told our story in our book, *Flip Your Classroom* (Bergmann & Sams, 2012). In a nutshell, we were trying to solve the problem of students who missed class and had a hard time making up the work. This led us to recording our in-class presentations. We soon realized that the best use of our face-to-face class time was not standing in front of students lecturing them; it was getting students actively engaged in learning. When we "flipped" our classes—that is, had students watch recorded lectures at home and work on live problem solving during class—we saw one standard deviation improvement in student achievement across the board.

During my second year of flipping, a transfer student joined my chemistry class at the semester break. She had no previous experience studying chemistry. When the counselor asked me whether Gisella could join the class, my initial reaction was to say no because she would be too far behind. She lacked all the critical knowledge and learning in chemistry that had taken place during the first semester—learning that had prepared the other students in the class to master the second semester's content.

But I had recorded all the lessons, and I had all the required activities. Why couldn't Gisella join the class and just start from the beginning? And so she did. I put her on an individual learning plan. While other students were working on second-semester material, Gisella was working on material from the first semester. I watched her learning progress and was amazed at how much and how quickly she learned. In fact, during that second semester, she completed about 80 percent of an entire year's worth of chemistry. I then realized that all students should have the freedom and opportunity that Gisella had enjoyed.

This led to a transformation in my entire notion of teaching and learning. Whereas I used to follow a rigid schedule and keep all my students on the same page at the same time, now I'm fine with students working on whatever it is that they need to learn, because I know they don't all learn at the same pace. I started reading the research on mastery learning and digging deep into what we know about learning in general. Instead of saying, "I taught it, and they didn't learn it," I now say, "If they didn't learn it, that's on *me*."

After using mastery learning for two years, my journey took a detour. The early work I did with the flipped learning movement, coupled with the success of *Flip Your Classroom,* steered me into district technology facilitation and, eventually, to work as an educational consultant. I had the privilege of sharing the power of flipped learning in schools all over the world. I visited schools in the United Arab Emirates, Spain, China, South Korea, Australia, Taiwan, New

Zealand, Iceland, Norway, Sweden, Brazil, Turkey, Jordan, Argentina, Mexico, the United Kingdom, and all over the United States.

But something nagged me. Even as I heard countless stories from educators about the positive effects of flipped learning, I found myself more and more disconnected from actual students. I came to realize that my life vision was to reach every student—not just as a speaker, an author, and a workshop leader, but as a teacher. To that end, I accepted a position at Houston Christian High School in Houston, Texas. This is now my third year back teaching science using mastery learning.

In preparation for writing this book, I talked with dozens of teachers and researchers who are implementing and studying mastery learning in a wide variety of classrooms and subjects. They are the true experts. Over the years, they have learned and improved on the flipped-mastery model. This book offers a valuable synthesis of their ideas, but also and most important, it shows you how to implement the approach with efficacy.

An Overview of the Book

Around the world, there are already thousands of teachers successfully implementing mastery learning. I have used the approach since 2009 in my classroom—and I've written this book to help you successfully implement mastery learning in yours. I want to challenge your thinking about what your students can and can't do, and at the same time, provide a practical, step-by-step guide that shows you how to teach using mastery learning.

The Mastery Learning Handbook consists of 16 short chapters divided into three parts:

- **Part 1** shows you how to prepare yourself and your classroom for a switch to mastery learning.
- **Part 2** leads you step by step through the mastery learning cycle. To get the most out of this book, you should create a mastery unit as you work through Part 2. I encourage you to adapt one unit of study in one class or subject that you teach. The unit should take between one and four weeks.
- **Part 3** guides you in implementing mastery learning. It covers the practical realities of a mastery learning classroom—what it looks like on the ground, how to manage assessments and grading, and how to deal with common issues that arise.

Let's get started.

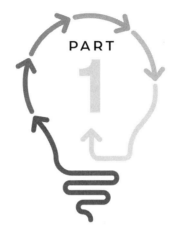

First Things First

1
The Promise of Mastery Learning

What is mastery learning? Here's the definition I've settled on:

> **mastery learning** (n.)—an approach to classroom instruction that empowers every student at every level to progress with confidence. The teacher uses flexible pacing to guide students through a cyclic process of preparation, demonstration of knowledge, and feedback until there is a mutual agreement between the teacher and individual student that the student is ready for the next cycle to begin.

Bob Furlong, a biology teacher at Otsego High School in Bowling Green, Ohio, has noted that he's sometimes uncomfortable using the term *mastery*. He says that what he's really doing is getting students to a certain level of proficiency. They aren't masters, technically, but they are able to demonstrate deep understanding of a topic. Likewise, when I teach high school science courses, I'm not creating "masters of science." But I do know how to get students to a good understanding of science. I know how to lead them to become informed and curious young people who can analyze and evaluate their learning. So, like Bob, although I'm not entirely comfortable with the term *mastery*, I'll nevertheless use it in this book.

Maybe you are thinking that what I'm describing sounds a lot like another approach you've heard of, something called *competency-based learning*. Researchers (Sturgis et al., 2011) at the Aurora Institute, formerly iNACOL, identified five key tenets of the approach:

- Students advance upon mastery.
- Competencies include explicit, measurable, and transferable learning objectives that empower students.
- Assessment is meaningful and a positive learning experience for students.

- Students receive timely, differentiated support based on their individual learning needs.
- Learning outcomes emphasize competencies that include the application and creation of knowledge, along with the development of important skills and dispositions. (p. 6)

This concise list is also a helpful description of mastery learning. Note that the word *mastery* even appears in the first bullet. So this book could actually have *competency* in its main title instead of *mastery*. If you are looking for a practical way to implement competency-based learning, this book will serve you as well.

A Brief History of Mastery Learning

At the turn of the last century, Carleton Washburne was growing up in a privileged neighborhood in Chicago, Illinois. He received a stellar education but didn't apply himself in the classroom. After college, faced with few job opportunities, he reluctantly became a teacher. His first post was in La Puente, California, in a community that was economically challenged. Instead of finding energized and inquisitive students, he found disengaged students for whom school was a perpetual struggle.

Washburne then began a quest to figure out how to reach his students. How could he help them get the amazing education he had received? In his search for answers, he went back to the work of Aristotle. In an Aristotelian education, learning is personalized for each learner. It focuses on the specific needs of each student and meets them just where they are.

Washburne spent the bulk of his life trying to implement this approach. As superintendent of Illinois's Winnetka Schools from 1919 to 1943, he began to implement mastery learning at scale, in what became known as the Winnetka Plan. In this plan, the curriculum was divided into two main sectors: "common essentials" and "creative group activities." The first sector consisted of spelling, reading, counting, and writing. Student learning paths were individualized, and students progressed at their own pace. They had to fully master each skill to move on to the next level, and they couldn't fail a grade. The creative group activities included art, literature, music, crafts, physical activities, and drama. These were ungraded, and students were encouraged to explore what interested them. There were no defined mastery objectives.

One of the key premises of the Winnetka Plan was that *all* students could learn, given enough time and support. In the late 1950s, the American educational psychologist Benjamin Bloom also promoted this approach. Sadly, mastery never really took hold in most schools. The logistics of running a mastery class proved too burdensome for the average teacher. And the current focus on testing makes things doubly difficult. In fact, according to Mark McCourt (2019), a leading authority on teaching for mastery, unless school leadership is willing to stop focusing on high-stakes tests, mastery learning is doomed to failure.

Nevertheless, I have met many flipped-mastery teachers—teachers who have flipped their classroom and are incorporating mastery learning—who are doing this on their own. These teachers are my heroes. They realize that reaching their students is their number-one priority and that mastery works. The reality is that all students can learn. And they can learn complex material. We just need to create the environment that will enable every student to reach mastery.

Does Mastery Learning Work?

To answer this question, we need to look at some research. In 1988, the research team of James Kulik and Chen-Lin Kulik did a meta-analysis of 108 studies on mastery learning. They found that mastery learning programs have "positive effects on examination performance of students in colleges, high schools, and the upper grades in elementary school." They also found that the "effects appear to be stronger on the weaker students in class." Finally, they determined that "mastery learning programs have positive effects on student attitudes toward course content" (p. 79). Their one caution is that mastery learning may reduce course completion rates in college classes.

More recently, in 2019, Dedi Kuswandi from the State University of Malang in Indonesia studied the effect of a flipped-mastery class assisted by social media on 61 engineering students. The experimental group scored 20 percent higher than the control group in a conventional learning setting. Kuswandi found that students were more motivated, came better prepared to class, felt less anxious, and had more fun learning.

Bob Furlong, the high school biology teacher I mentioned earlier, uses mastery learning in his classroom. He works in a Title I school, where many students come from disadvantaged backgrounds. Before I show you Bob's results, let me address something. You might be wondering how students with limited access to technology fare in a mastery model. Although there are indeed barriers to overcome in economically challenged communities with limited access to technology and high-speed internet access, many teachers have found creative workarounds. Some ask students do much of the prework on mobile devices. Others provide extra time in their classrooms for the prework. I have also seen entire schools carve out time during resource periods for students to access the prelearning material via the school's infrastructure and devices.

Back to Bob. His state, Ohio, administers end-of-course exams in a variety of subjects and uses a complex algorithm that predicts student performance on those exams. Figure 1.1 shows that Bob's biology students outperformed expectations, demonstrating the efficacy of mastery learning.

Figure 1.1 End-of-Course (EOC) Results for Bob Furlong's Mastery Students

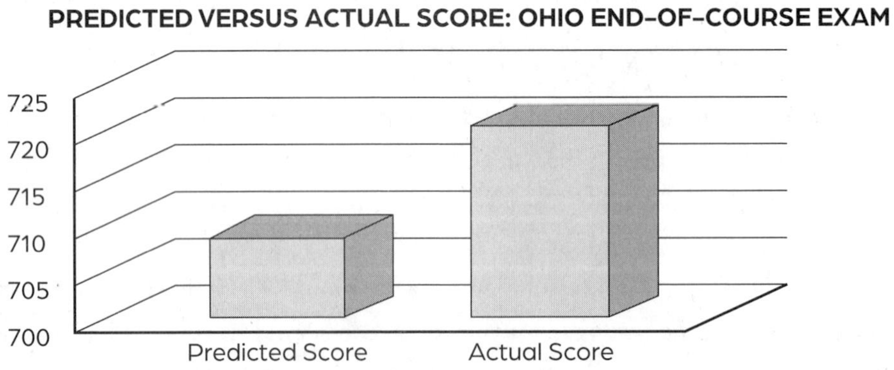

Bloom and the 2 Sigma Problem

In 1984, Bloom published an article in *Educational Researcher* titled "The 2 Sigma Problem: The Search for Methods of Group Instruction as Effective as One-to-One Tutoring." He cited studies that compared student achievement under conventional teaching, mastery learning, and one-to-one tutoring. Figure 1.2 shows that distribution. The research indicates that one-to-one tutoring produces a two standard deviation (2 sigma) improvement over the average of the control class (conventional teaching), whereas mastery learning results in students performing 1 sigma above the average of the control class.

Figure 1.2 Benjamin Bloom's 2 Sigma Graph

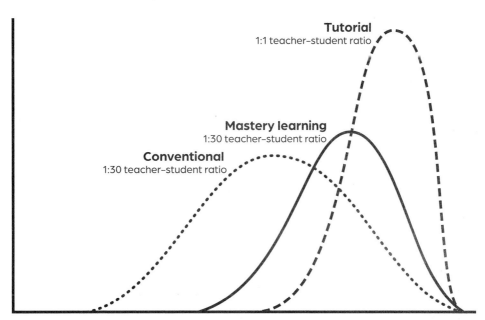

Source: From "The 2 Sigma Problem: The Search for Methods of Group Instruction as Effective as One-to-One Tutoring," by B. S. Bloom, 1984, *Educational Researcher, 13*(6), p. 25. Copyright 1984 by SAGE Publications. Reprinted with permission.

The question Bloom posed in his article was this: "Can researchers and teachers devise teaching-learning conditions that will enable the majority of students under *group instruction* to attain levels of achievement that can at present be reached only under good tutoring conditions?" (pp. 4–5).

I believe that the flipped-mastery model can create just those conditions. If you walk into a flipped-mastery class, you'll find an environment that allows for a lot of individual and small-group tutoring, with mastery learning at its core. These classrooms are not only helping students achieve academically but also enabling teachers to meet more of their students' social and emotional needs.

If mastery learning is such a powerful learning strategy, why hasn't it been more widely adopted? After all, none other than Benjamin Bloom showed just how effective it could be. In many ways, Bloom's ideas needed some logistical support. He never quite solved two big problems:

- When does a teacher do direct instruction if students are all working on different levels of content?

- How can teachers manage multiple assessments? That is, how many versions of an exam would they need to have on file, and how would they find the time to grade them?

Fortunately, technology has overcome these hurdles. Teachers can now time-shift direct instruction through the use of assigned videos and readings. And online assessments now allow for thousands of versions of exams that assess the same learning objectives. With some of these hurdles behind us, let's look at what characterizes mastery learning.

What Mastery Learning Looks Like

Frankly, the best way to understand this model would be to visit a flipped-mastery classroom. However, in lieu of that, let's take a 30,000-foot view of what you might see there. You would notice the following:

- **An absence of whole-class direct instruction.** Direct instruction still occurs, but it occurs in a flipped manner, with students watching videos or reading as prework.
- **A flexible pace.** Not every student is on the same page; students move through the curriculum at the level appropriate for them.
- **Extreme differentiation.** I talk with every student in every class every day, and by doing so, I'm able to customize the learning path of each student. This is especially crucial in a post-pandemic world where students are returning to school with such a wide discrepancy of experiences.
- **Multiple teacher-student interactions.** I continually walk around the classroom interacting with students—always in formative assessment mode—checking for understanding, asking questions, and having students ask questions of me.
- **Student collaboration.** Although each student is on their own individual learning path, they work collaboratively with their peers to learn.
- **Multiple versions of assessments.** Each time students take a summative assessment, they get a different test. The D2L Brightspace quizzing feature (see www.d2l.com/brightspace) enables me to have thousands of versions of the same test; the different questions assess the same objectives.
- **Immediate teacher feedback.** When students complete a summative assessment, we score it together. If they are successful, I ring a gong and

we celebrate. If they aren't, I use the session as remedial time to help them prepare to retake the assessment.
- **A focus on relationships.** With the extra time available to interact, mastery teachers have more time to develop positive relationships with students. We all know that students learn best when their teacher isn't just interested in their academic achievement but, instead, is their coach and cheerleader. Believing in students is always the best policy.
- **Summative assessments.** In my class, I expect students to score at least 80 percent on all summative assessments. Many students take these multiple times until they achieve mastery.
- **Social justice and equity.** Research has shown that mastery learning has its greatest effect on students at risk of academic failure (Ironsmith & Eppler, 2007). At some point, mastery learning is an equity issue, because it helps the students who need the most support.

Mastery learning shows great promise to fundamentally change the nature of how we educate. This is a necessary shift. And the good news is that any teacher can do it.

The Changing Role of the Teacher

Embracing a mastery model means rethinking the teacher's role in the classroom. Alicia Schreiber, a lead teacher in New Zealand, shared five ways that her role has changed since she adopted a mastery-based approach:

- **Time.** You have to invest your time differently with this approach. You have to commit to checking in with every student every day. No longer can you just stand and deliver and hope for the best.
- **Purpose.** Ask yourself the purpose of this lesson. What are the most important things you want students to know and be able to do? Mastery teachers are clear about what demonstrates mastery in each lesson.
- **Contextual learning.** You need to connect your content to the lives of your students. What about your curriculum threads into their lives? Do your students understand how each lesson fits into the whole?
- **Active teaching.** You now will rove around your classroom instead of standing at the front. You will make on-the-spot decisions about who to help and who not to help. You will be the director of a classroom instead

of the main actor. As such, you'll suddenly experience those magical moments where everything comes together and students learn deeply.
- **Relationships.** Connecting with students is job number one. You need to be willing to enter into the messiness of their lives. Because you have more time to spend with your students, you'll get to know them better—not just their cognitive needs, but their affective needs as well. Be ready.

We've touched on the importance of mastery learning and on the changing role of the teacher. But why is it so important to implement now?

The Right Strategy for the Right Time

Let's look at four reasons why you should consider implementing mastery learning at this moment in time.

You will reach your struggling students

Bob Furlong teaches an on-level biology class that is made up of students who struggle. He has found that mastery learning works best with this group. When he first introduced the approach to his struggling learners, they didn't believe he was really on their side. These students felt that school was out to get them; they were waiting for the "gotcha" moment when everything would come crashing down on them. But as the weeks went by, they realized they could trust Mr. Furlong; they began to relax and get down to the process of really learning. The students found that mastery provided them with a safety net and helped them become more successful learners, significantly outperforming students in other districts with similar demographics. As Bob said, "I can never go back. This simply works."

You will reach your high-achieving students

One question I kept asking mastery teachers as I was compiling information for this book was this: How do you challenge your high-achieving students? I was asking because I saw huge benefits for my struggling students, but not as many for my more able ones.

The good news is that many of the educators I spoke with have used mastery learning to crack the code to reaching high achievers. In Chapter 14, we'll go deeper into some specific strategies. As a teaser, Hassan Wilson's students declare majors, Bob Furlong has an "*A* option," and Holly Stuart uses a unique grid system that grades students on improvement.

You will be better equipped to teach in a post–COVID world

Natalie Victorov, a 4th grade teacher in Freeport, Illinois, shared just how hard the COVID-19 pandemic has been on her students. The school provided packets for students every two weeks to help keep them on track. But in her high-needs school, some parents didn't pick up the packets, and some students lost them. Even Natalie, a master teacher, struggled to reach her students. Some students came back to school with little learning loss, but many came back with significant gaps.

The beauty of mastery learning is that students don't need to be on the same page at the same time. This is crucial, because given our experience with the pandemic, many students are woefully behind, and teachers need a solution that will help them all succeed. You can implement mastery learning in the traditional structure of the everyday classroom. You don't have to reinvent the structure of school. You don't have to change the schedule. You don't have to change the day-to-day operations of the school. You can implement mastery learning one class at a time.

Your students will love you for it

As part of the research for this book, I asked each mastery learning teacher I interviewed to send me examples of student feedback. Here's a sample of what their students had to say about the experience of mastery learning:

- "Thanks for helping me grow up a bit and be independent."
- "I really enjoyed this course this year. The self-pacing was fun, and I loved the system you use."
- "Before this year, I never really enjoyed science, and it was never one of my favorite classes. But this year, science was probably my favorite class."
- "I'm really sad to leave this class. I loved our conversations with you. Don't forget to B. cereus!"
- "Mastery-flipped learning has assisted me with my learning because it's given me a basis of knowledge and understanding before we review the concept in class. This technique is helpful to consolidate understanding content. It also helps me with responsibility and independence."

Here are some comments I gathered from my own students:

- "Mastery learning helps me feel way more confident in my ability to learn the material and takes away so much stress and anxiety that I would have on a test without it. I still worry about tests, but with mastery learning, I don't have the usual test anxiety."
- "I know that I will fully comprehend the material without being punished for not learning it in a short amount of time. I get to learn at my own pace."
- "I am able to really enjoy the material and see the benefits of it without the fast-paced anxiousness of a normal classroom."
- "Mastery learning has been very positive for me. Because we are able to retake tests, the world isn't over if I don't do well on one. Because of this environment, I am able to actually focus on learning the content, and we are able to go at the pace we need. In other classes, it's assumed that everyone learns at the same pace."

These comments reveal a number of common themes:

- Students like having autonomy and choices.
- Students feel less pressure to perform and report lower levels of anxiety about a mastery course.
- Students believe that mastery learning is a better reflection of their learning.
- Students feel more connected to their teachers.
- Students feel they do a better job of learning the content.

These are pretty convincing arguments for mastery learning.

The Challenge of Changing Your Mindset

Before we end this chapter, I want to acknowledge how hard it can be to shift one's mindset.

Like me, many of you learned how to teach during the last century. You were taught how to craft the best presentation, the best assessments, and the best classroom management plan. My formation as a teacher relied heavily on Madeline Hunter's lesson design plan, which involved the anticipatory set, the introduction of new material, guided practice, independent practice, and closure. I had to be in total control of the learning process. All my students worked on the same thing, and we kept together. When students fell behind, I encouraged them to come in for extra help. But invariably, some students were lost in the shuffle. Sadly, I sometimes even blamed the students, thinking, "I taught it to them, but they didn't learn it."

For me, the mindset change happened when I decided to interview my students during a culminating end-of-year project. I asked a few fundamental questions of each student, and I was dismayed at how few of them really understood what I had taught. Even some students with high grades were lost when I asked them to expound on the basic building blocks of my course.

You may wonder, as I did, whether your students, like mine, just memorized items for the test and then promptly forgot everything.

If you decide to go down this rabbit hole of mastery learning, you and your teaching will be forever changed. But this will require a few shifts in your thinking. First, you will have to be fine with giving up some of the control of your class. I know this is no small thing. I used to be the control-freak teacher who made sure that all students were doing exactly what I wanted. I was proud of the fact that I was a bell-to-bell teacher. No wasted time in my class! But when I gave up some—some, not all—of the control, I was blown away by how my students took more ownership of their learning, by how they began to enjoy learning with more autonomy. All my metrics rose dramatically. Student test scores rose, and, better yet, when I interviewed the students at the end of the year, most of them really knew the big ideas.

Second, I had to be OK with not being the center of attention. Before flipped learning, and especially mastery learning, I loved to be the smart guy who gave engaging and scintillating lectures. The fact is, I'm a good speaker. I've given a TED Talk, and I've spoken to thousands of people at once. But in my classroom, I don't use my speaking skills anymore because mastery learning just works. I still believe in the power of a clear and engaging lecture, but I don't deliver these in my class. I save them for my flipped videos. If you love being professorial and the center of attention, this will be hard for you. It was for me.

Last, you will have to rethink what you believe about grading and assessment. I used to believe in points and percentages. If a student got 89.4 percent, that was a *B*. They had one chance to prove they had mastered something; if they didn't perform on the day of the test, well, too bad. But now I don't care *when* students learn something; I just care that they learn it. We shouldn't penalize students who process slowly. Slow processing isn't a mark of low intelligence. In fact, it may be a mark of deeper understanding.

So, are *you* up for the challenge? Are you ready to rethink what class could be like if you let go of some of the control? Are you going to be OK with not being the center of attention? Are you willing to let go of your notions of what it means to be intelligent? And are you frustrated that, despite the effort you're putting in now, all your students aren't learning as well as they could?

If so, read on!

2

Setting the Stage for Mastery Learning

You've made it to Chapter 2, so you must be, at a minimum, intrigued. You have some hope that your classroom could look and fundamentally *be* different. You want to get to the nitty-gritty details of how you might make mastery learning a reality. This chapter will get you started.

The Role of Flipped Learning

This is a book on mastery learning, but I have found that when mastery learning is done in conjunction with flipped learning, it's much more successful.

I know there are teachers out there who are hesitant about using flipped learning, and if you're one of them, stick with me for a bit. You may think that flipped learning means that students simply watch videos before class. If so, this section will dispel that misconception. And if you still hesitate to use elements of flipped learning as you move to mastery learning, that's OK. This book will guide you through the steps to mastery learning implementation in a way that will still be quite effective.

So why do I say that flipped learning plays a valuable role in mastery learning? As you may recall from the last chapter, there are two significant barriers to implementing mastery learning. The first has to do with direct instruction: When do you do it? Flipped learning solves this problem. Having students interact with lower-level tasks ahead of time increases your ability to make mastery learning work.

In my book *Solving the Homework Problem by Flipping the Learning* (Bergmann, 2017), I give a quick summary of flipped learning. Here is an excerpt that introduces an important idea explained in that book:

Flipped learning, at its core, is a very simple idea: direct instruction and basic content delivery is delivered to students through an instructional video (which I will call a flipped video) or a text assignment outside class time, and then class time is devoted to application, analysis, and practice, with the teacher present to clear up misconceptions and questions. Basically, the easy stuff is done before the face-to-face class time. Once the teacher and students are in the same room, the basic content has been introduced, and the repurposed class time is used to engage students in higher-order thinking. The students do the easy stuff before class and the hard stuff in class, where the teacher is there to help them. (pp. 11–12)

Flipped learning can best be summarized by redrawing Bloom's taxonomy pyramid as a diamond (see Figure 2.1).

Figure 2.1 Bloom's Taxonomy Diamond

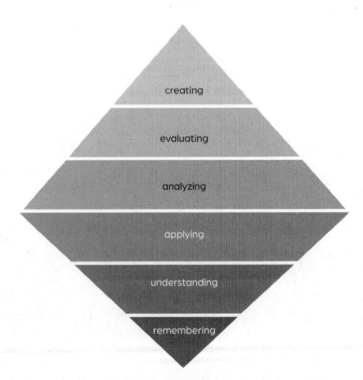

Source: From *Solving the Homework Problem by Flipping the Learning* (p. 10), by J. Bergmann, 2017, ASCD. Copyright 2017 by ASCD.

The "easy stuff"—remembering and understanding—sits at the lower levels of Bloom's taxonomy, and the "hard stuff"—applying, analyzing, evaluating, and creating—moves progressively upward. The area of the diamond represents the rough percentage of class time you should spend on each. Notice that the diamond is widest in the center, indicating that teachers should arrange for students to spend a substantial amount of time applying and analyzing.

Of course, the reality is that most students spend most of their class time at the bottom of Bloom's taxonomy, and teachers send the hard work of applying and analyzing home, where students may not be able to access the help and guidance they need to do it or even a quiet space in which to concentrate. It's an arrangement that ensures at least some students will miss out on the desired learning and fall further and further behind.

Flipped educators distinguish between what we call *independent space* and *group space*. In independent space, students work alone with the content and are introduced to a new topic. This comes through watching a flipped video or reading a given text. Although this arrangement may sound isolating, there are multiple ways to make this asynchronous experience social. In group space, students work together on projects, assignments, or other learning activities. These might be whole-class activities such as debates, experiments, or Socratic dialogues.

Bloom's taxonomy acts as a filter for deciding which activities to do in the group space and which activities to do in the independent space. The easy stuff (remembering and understanding) happens in the independent space, and the hard stuff (applying, analyzing, evaluating, and creating) takes place in the group space, where the teacher is present to help all students navigate complex material.

Keep these two terms, *independent space* and *group space,* in mind as we progress through the book. I will use them as we plan for mastery learning, create meaningful mastery lessons, and assess student learning.

Begin with the End in Mind

The ideal way to plan for mastery learning is to use a backward design process. Maybe, like me, you weren't taught how to plan backward. When I first started teaching in 1986, I was handed a textbook and told to teach it. That textbook was my curriculum. I used it to determine what and how to teach. I started by designing lessons that I thought would be engaging, and after I had taught a chapter, I would write a test to assess what my students had learned.

By now, most educators are at least somewhat familiar with the seminal work done by Grant Wiggins and Jay McTighe. Their book *Understanding by Design* (2005) introduced the world to the idea of *backward design*, a planning framework that flips my old planning process on its head. It asks us to start not with the lessons but rather with the overall goals: the outcomes we want students to achieve.

Backward design has three stages (McTighe, 2020):

- **Identify desired results.**
  —What are the learning objectives and enduring understandings?
  —What are the essential questions?
- **Determine acceptable evidence.**
  —How will you know if your students have achieved the desired results?
  —What performance tasks can students complete to demonstrate their mastery?
- **Plan learning experiences and instruction.**
  —What teaching and learning experiences can you design that will help students achieve the desired results?

When I first started using mastery learning, I was unaware of backward design, so I planned lessons and then built the assessments. But in doing it that way, I created a lot of frustration for both me and my students. Only some of my students were mastering the material, meaning my system was flawed. And since most assessments were high-stakes tests, the students were frustrated and stressed. If you're going to really benefit from this book, I recommend using backward design in your planning process.

Think *Cyclical,* Not Linear

As I interviewed people for this book, actual teachers using mastery learning, I began to see a pattern. We were all creating *cyclical* patterns of learning instead of linear patterns. We chunked our curricula into smaller pieces and made room for remediation and discovery.

One mistake I used to make all the time, and frankly still make to some extent, is thinking too linearly about my units of study. In my old-school mind, I had constructed set of units of study filled mostly with stuff for my students to learn. They didn't contain much in terms of thinking skills or authentic tasks; essentially, they just covered the content in the textbook.

Mastery teachers do so much more than guide students through the content of a textbook. They set up mastery cycles of learning that roll back on themselves. Students move through the curriculum at flexible paces, and if they don't master the material, they cycle back to some sort of remediation and support structure that enables them to master it.

Another reason that mastery cycles are important is that they chunk the course material into smaller, bite-sized pieces, allowing students to accomplish something in a relatively short amount of time. This is an important point. When the chunks are just the right size (length), students feel a great sense of accomplishment; for students who tend to struggle, this can be a powerful motivator. Almost to a person, the experts I connected with set mastery cycles that last between two and three weeks. Two teachers go so far as exclusively using one-week cycles.

When I use the term *cycle*, I'm referring to the mastery learning cycle shown in Figure 2.2 (see p. 24). You start with clear objectives, then you create your mastery rubric, then you plan your assessments, then you get into the nitty-gritty of lesson planning, then you assess student learning, and then, at the end, you provide remediation. As we progress through the book, you will learn how to create each of the elements listed in the cycle. You might notice that the Assess category differs in presentation from the rest; this is simply to indicate that assessment occurs in different spots in the cycle, depending on whose point of view you take. From the students' perspective, summative assessment happens toward the end of the cycle; for the teacher who is doing the planning, it's addressed early in the cycle, as with backward design.

You may not need to adjust the current way you plan. You likely already have clear learning objectives. You likely already have a library of engaging activities. You likely already have created some assessments. And you likely already have notes on your direct instruction, perhaps in the form of some sort of presentation software, such as PowerPoint. The trick is to put these learning components together into the mastery learning cycle.

Perhaps the one piece you're missing is a remediation plan. What will you do for those students who don't get the material on the first go-around? The answer doesn't have to be complicated. I typically score my students' summative assessments in their presence, and during that session, it's relatively easy for me to see if a student shows any patterns of misconception or misunderstanding. I then go over that missing piece and send the student back to try and answer a few other questions related to that issue before they retake the mastery assessment.

Figure 2.2 The Mastery Learning Cycle

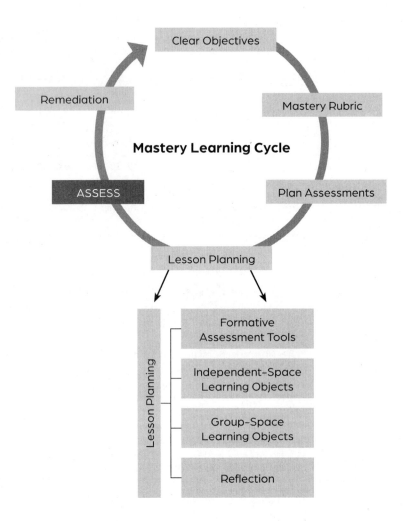

3

Creating Mastery Spaces

Because mastery learning changes how you teach and how your students learn, it's no surprise that you'll need to change your classroom setup.

Most classrooms are designed for the teacher to talk to students from the front of the room. Perhaps yours is set up for presentations, with an interactive whiteboard front and center and your students' desks all facing forward. But when you embrace mastery learning, you significantly reduce, if not eliminate, the need for whole-group instruction. Gone are the days when you want students to sit in rows and focus solely on you and "your teaching."

The Mastery-Friendly Classroom

What can you do to make your classroom more conducive to mastery learning? One way to look at this is to think of your room as a series of stations. Elementary school teachers do this all the time; they understand the idea of a station rotation model. With mastery learning, you're essentially going to set up your room with several stations, providing different areas where students can assemble depending on whether they're working in a group, taking an assessment, doing remedial work, or finishing up a project on their own.

What's that? What if you don't have the budget to rearrange your classroom, or you share a room with a colleague who is not into mastery? Or your room has desks that are bolted to the floor and can't be moved? If this is the case, it's about doing the best you can and moving kids rather than furniture. I'll talk more about this in a page or two.

To kick things off, though, here are three good, general guidelines.

Keep things flexible

Can you quickly switch your classroom learning space to adapt to a variety of learning modalities (e.g., collaborative group work, individual work, Socratic circles, small-group tutorials)? Because different activities are going to happen at different times, keeping things flexible can greatly maximize learning. Ideally, you should be able to rearrange your furniture on the fly. One easy way to do this is to have furniture with wheels. School furniture now comes in a variety of shapes that can serve as individual stations and then can quickly be transformed into collaborative spaces. Such a setup also sends a message that learning will be different in this space.

Set up the space for active learning

If you were to walk into an active learning classroom, what might you see? Here's a sampling:

- Students solving problems in collaborative groups, processing together
- Students discussing and debating issues brought up in the class
- Students doing hands-on and minds-on activities
- Students looking up information on the internet

To foster these activities, arrange desks in collaborative pods as opposed to in rows. Setting up your room for active learning is key. How you accomplish this is up to you and your creativity.

What about the teacher in such a classroom? You're much less likely to find them in the traditional "teacher spot," at the front of the classroom, than to spot them roaming around the room, working individually or in small groups with their students.

Arrange your room with student choice and student ownership in mind

Do students have choices in how they use the learning space? Can they choose which portion of the space they want to use for a specific task? Does your classroom enable students to drive their own learning? Do they have choices about when and how they learn? Do they have choices about how they can demonstrate what they have learned? When students know they have more choice in how they learn, they are more likely to learn.

Aligning Your Space with Mastery Learning

With the general guidelines laid out, let's turn to some specific suggestions for aligning your classroom space with the mastery learning approach.

Expand your whiteboard spaces

Classrooms rarely have enough whiteboard space. In my room, my tables now have whiteboard surfaces. There's nothing like a group of students working together with a dry-erase marker in hand. I even encourage students to write on my black lab tables with liquid chalk. Many teachers have several small, portable dry-erase boards that individual students can use. You can purchase them from vendors or make them inexpensively by cutting up sheets of whiteboard material available from your local big-box store.

Offer multiple levels

When considering room design, we often think exclusively in terms of the horizontal. I visited a mastery classroom where the teacher had a mixture of levels. Some students stood at genius bar–height tables, whereas others lounged close to the ground on beanbag chairs. The teacher found that students migrated to different spaces depending on what worked best for them.

Give each space a purpose

I have segmented my classroom into spaces for students to work individually or in small groups on more paper-focused work. I offer other spaces for hands-on activities. And I have designated another area for assessments. I have also seen teachers set up areas for small-group tutorials, a studio for students to create videos, a makerspace for student projects, and a quiet space for individual work.

Remember that bins are your friends

If you're like me, you teach a variety of courses in the same room. If you move from room to room, organizing all the class materials can be daunting. My simple solution is to use large bins that each contain a given activity, and I label them accordingly. I put all the necessary equipment, papers, and tools in the bin, and students know to put everything back the way they found it. For me as a science teacher, these bins contain things like beakers, rulers, and chemicals. But they also might contain scissors, colored pencils, and other items that will promote active learning. I stack the bins on a cart or in a corner of the room so I can quickly switch to a different task or activity between classes.

Keeping Students on Task

I started teaching with mastery learning in a high school chemistry class, arguably the most dangerous class taught at our school. In light of that, setting up multiple labs for students to work on in a single class period might seem crazy. I've since come to believe that it's actually a safer way to go. On any given day, I might have three different experiments set up in my room. But only about half of my students are doing a lab at a time. And one requirement I have before students engage in an experiment is that I spend time with each group discussing the lab and going over safety measures. Each of these discussions probably takes about five minutes, and I work with small groups of no more than six students.

I've found this approach far superior to giving instructions to a whole class of students and then trying to get them started. When I taught traditionally, some students listened to the pre-lab instructions and others didn't. And when they got started on the lab, many students turned to their peers and asked, "Do you know what to do?" But when I'm looking in the eyes of four students and we're discussing what those four students need to do, they're much more attentive.

This also helps me monitor students who might have a tendency to get off task. This was brought home to me last year when I was teaching during the pandemic. We met in person for part of the year, and because we were behind in our curriculum, I decided to have all students do the same lab on the same day in class. Very old-school. One of my off-task students decided it would be a good idea to pour boiling water on another kid. In a mastery class, where only a small portion of students would be doing the experiment, this would not have happened.

Sample Room Configurations from Mastery Teachers

Let's look at how some of our expert mastery learning teachers have designed their rooms. They represent different grade levels and subject areas: a middle school science classroom, a lower elementary classroom, a 4th grade classroom, and a high school science classroom.

As you can see in Figure 3.1, six small circular desks occupy the center of Hassan Wilson's classroom. Both visually and strategically, this arrangement puts the focus on individual and small-group work, on students doing different things at the same time.

Figure 3.1 Hassan Wilson's Room: Middle School Science

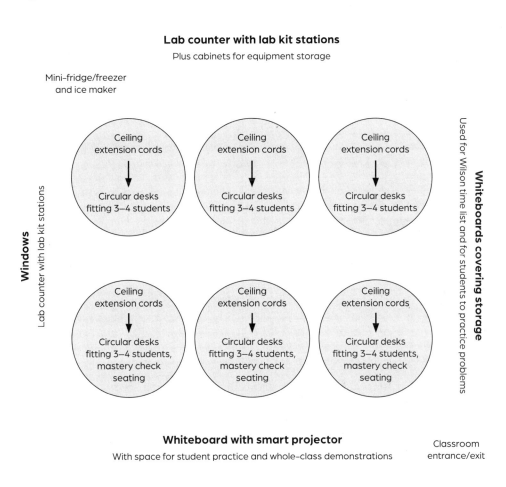

Alicia Schreiber's room (shown in Figure 3.2, see p. 30) is furnished with a variety of tables of different sizes and shapes. It's conducive to a teacher circulating around the classroom, stopping to engage with different groups of students. There's also a low table/floor area for students to work in, as well as a larger workshop group area.

Figure 3.2 Alicia Schreiber's Room: Lower Elementary

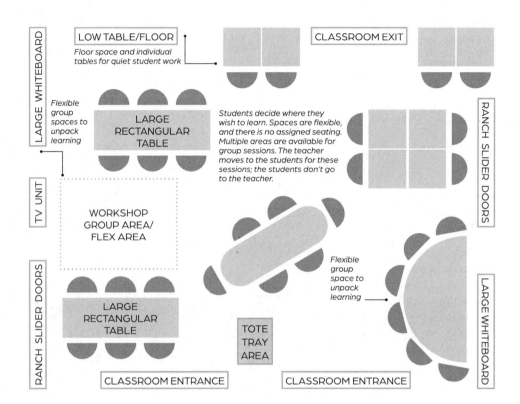

Hannah Curran's classroom offers another interesting configuration (see Figure 3.3). A group rug is the focal point of the room. It's surrounded by four desk arrangements, each featuring a standing desk. There are two countertops for group collaboration, and beanbag chairs offer flexible seating. The learning space also includes a calm corner where students can go when they need to regulate their emotions. Hannah's classroom has lots of flexibility and spaces for students to choose how to best work.

Nikki Conyers, a high school science teacher in New Zealand, has limited flexibility in her room. Student desks are in rows, and there's no space to move them. There's also no dedicated station space available, so Nikki created stations by posting station information on the walls of the surrounds.

Figure 3.3 Hannah Curran's Room: 4th Grade

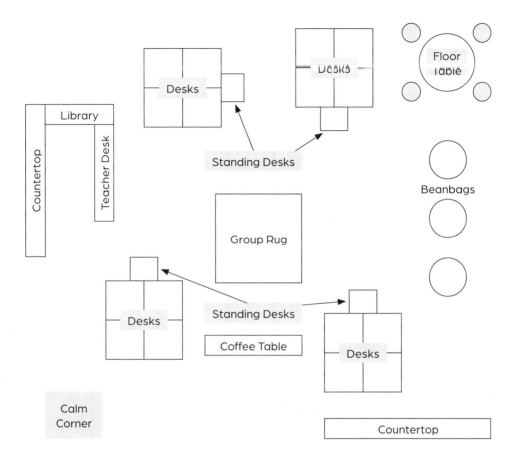

And what about my own classroom? Figure 3.4 (see p. 32) shows how I like to set it up.

As you can see, my room has a lot of fixed furniture. As a traditional science classroom, it doesn't offer much flexibility. There are whiteboards around the room, and my school purchased stick-on whiteboard material for the tables in the middle. We use the fixed lab tables for stations, which usually contain a variety of experiments set up for mastery learning. In the summative stations, students do their assessments on devices, with their screens always facing into the classroom so I can quickly check for integrity issues. Not pictured is a rolling whiteboard for students to collaborate around.

Ultimately you have to look at your own room and decide how to best use the space. It's ideal to have some flexibility there, but if you don't, then it's time to get creative. If you'd like feedback on how to revamp your space, I encourage you to ask in the community section of my website, JonBergmann.com. There, other mastery learning experts will help you brainstorm various ways you might set up your room.

Figure 3.4 Jon's Room: High School Science

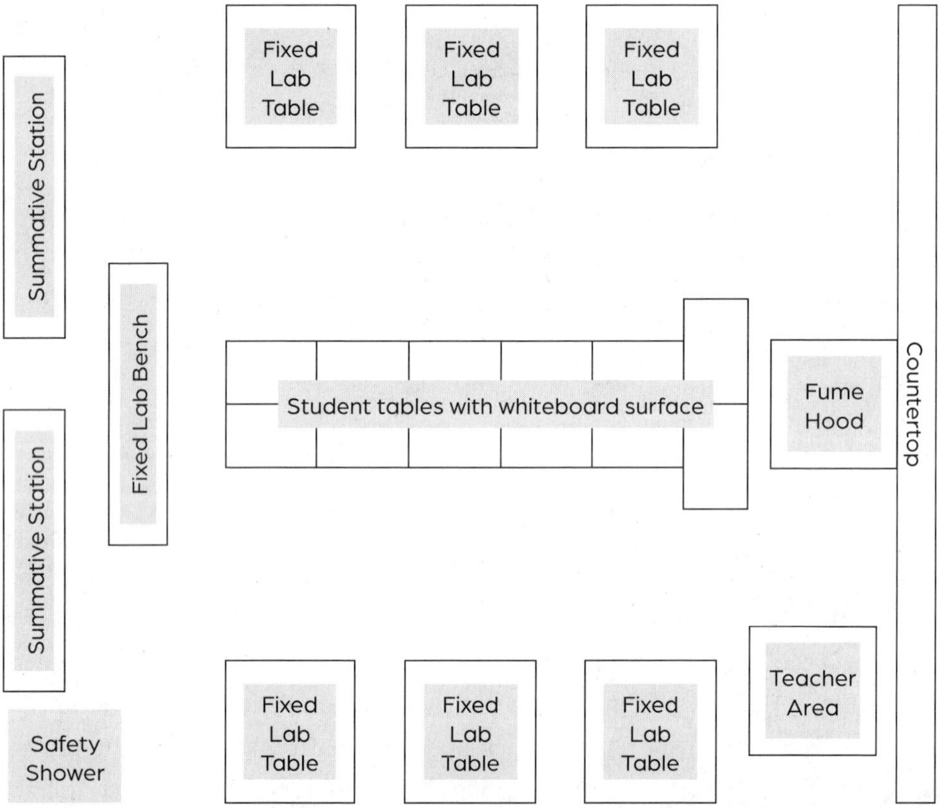

Planning for Mastery Learning

4
Big Picture Planning

Planning for mastery learning relies on the mastery learning cycle, introduced in Chapter 2 (see Figure 4.1 for a reminder).

Figure 4.1 The Mastery Learning Cycle

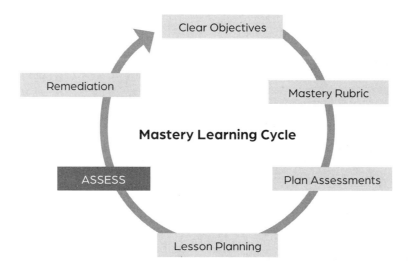

The cycle starts with setting clear objectives, and then it calls on the teacher to create a mastery rubric and an assessment plan, to pre-test, to plan lessons, to administer summative assessments, and to offer remediation. In this overview chapter, I want to provide a top-level look at each of these components.

- **Set clear objectives.** These are what you want students to know or be able to do. It's often best to state them in the form of essential questions.

- **Develop a mastery rubric.** How will you know how much each student has mastered? For many of you, this will be a new part of lesson planning.
- **Create an assessment plan.** How will you assess your students? Will you use a traditional test? Will you use an alternative form of assessment, such as a project, a video, or an authentic task? With backward design in mind, note that you will plan assessments *first* and actually assess students later on.
- **Pre-test your students.** What questions will reveal student understandings in this unit? Might a practical activity reveal more than a traditional test?
- **Plan your lessons.** How will you plan and chunk your lessons? Lesson planning encompasses four main elements: independent-space learning objects, group-space learning objects, formative assessments, and a reflection piece. We will look at these in more depth in the chapters that follow.
- **Administer summative assessments.** Remember, you have already designed your assessments earlier on in the cycle. But how will you manage having students taking tests at different times? How will you deal with multiple versions of tests, and how will you ensure test security? We will address these issues in Chapter 11.
- **Create a remediation plan.** How will you assist students who do not meet the minimum mastery learning level? Your plan should spell this out.

The Mastery Unit Planning Template

The Mastery Unit Planning Template shown in Figure 4.2 will guide you in this process. You can find an editable version of the template at this book's companion website, **TheMasteryLearningHandbook.com.** Don't start filling it out just yet, but do have it handy so that you can use it as you progress through the book.

Many of you may have your own way of planning, but I encourage you to follow this template as a learning exercise. Then, as you start your own mastery learning classroom, you can modify and adapt it to meet your needs. The mastery teachers I interviewed for this book all had different workflows. I have blended their ideas with mine to create this template, so it should prove useful.

Within the pages of the book, I'll be modeling how to complete the planning template with a unit on volcanoes that I use with my high school students. Additional completed planning template examples from a variety of classes, subjects, and levels are available at TheMasteryLearningHandbook.com.

Figure 4.2 Mastery Unit Planning Template

Unit Title:

Driving Question(s)

Clear Unit Objectives/Essential Questions

Mastery Rubric

Lesson	Proof of Basic Understanding "I sort of get it."	Proof of Clear Understanding "I get it."	Proof of Deeper Understanding "I really get it."
1			
2			
...			

Summative Assessment Plan

Pre-test Plan (if needed)

Lesson Planning

Lesson Title	Lesson Objective	Independent-Space Objects	Group-Space Objects	Formative Assessment Tools
1				
2				
...				

Reflection Plan

Remediation Plan

5

Developing Clear Objectives and the Mastery Rubric

The two steps in developing a mastery cycle are to determine clear objectives and create the mastery rubric. Let's look at each of these in more detail.

Setting Clear Objectives

To begin with, you need to determine what you want students to know or be able to do. You may have little control over this; you probably have a curriculum guide or a set of standards you have to follow. If you're in the United States, you might refer to the Common Core State Standards or to your individual state standards. If you teach outside the United States, you most likely have some governmental body that publishes standards.

Keep the following guidelines in mind as you do this work.

Start with driving questions

With those standards in mind, I encourage you to develop either one or several driving questions. This is the big idea of your unit. For example, here are two driving questions for this chapter of the book: *How do you develop clear objectives? How do you develop the mastery rubric?* The process of developing these questions can be powerful because it helps you and ultimately your students to see the big picture.

Frankly, in the past, I haven't been all that good at planning with backward design and using driving questions. Moreover, as I did the research for this book, I realized I wanted to make some changes in how I plan and deliver mastery to my students. So I now invite you into my head as I develop a driving question for my science class and go about building a unit with my resources.

Right now, I have on my computer screen a copy of my assigned textbook, a copy of the standards for Texas, and my old unit on volcanoes. Please go ahead and gather all the materials *you* will need to plan your unit. Those might include the textbook, a curriculum guide, and your old lesson plans.

As I look at the Texas standards, I notice that they're too vague and broad to help me design the unit on volcanoes. Thus, I use my expertise, the textbook's stated objectives, and some internet searches to come up with the following driving question: *What are the types, causes, and effects of volcanic activity on Earth?* This question is broad and gets at the heart of what students should know about volcanoes. It's a bit low on Bloom's taxonomy, but, as you will see in the unit plan, students will have plenty of opportunities to go deeper with the content.

Now I want you to come up with your own driving question for your unit. Add your question or questions in the designated place in the template.

Make standards accessible for students

To develop a good driving question, I often just put the standard into simpler language. I learned this from Andrew Swan, a middle school history teacher in Massachusetts. In my interview with him, he told me how he translates standards into kid-friendly language. Figure 5.1 shows one of his "translations."

Figure 5.1 Rephrased Standard from the Massachusetts Curriculum Framework for History and Social Science

Standard	Kid-Friendly Version
8.T2.1 Apply knowledge of the history of the American Revolutionary period to determine the experiences and events that led the colonists to declare independence; explain the key ideas about equality, representative government, limited government, rule of law, natural rights, common good, and the purpose of government in the Declaration of Independence.	• I can explain how certain events caused many American colonists to want independence from Britain. • I can explain several key ideas that appear in the Declaration of Independence.

Source: Massachusetts Department of Education, 2018, p. 105.

Andrew's "kid-friendly" standards may seem a little vague. However, he does this by design, noting that "I've painted myself into a corner so many times by being overly specific in the past." Flexibility in the standard allows him greater degrees of differentiation with students of varying readiness levels. And flexibility is paramount for Andrew. Some of his middle school students are ready for high school work, whereas others are at a 3rd grade reading level. It's not uncommon for 25 percent of Andrew's students to start out well below average. His goal is to have every student show learning progress, and he wants his standard to allow for that.

Develop essential questions and essential tasks

You've already listed the driving question for your unit in the template. If you recall, this was mine: *What are the types, causes, and effects of volcanic activity on Earth?* Now you need to develop some *essential questions* and tasks. Essential questions are much more detailed than driving questions, and they provide specific assessment criteria that you can easily measure. Although you may have one or two driving questions, you might have many essential questions or tasks.

Let's go back inside my head as I develop the essential questions for my volcano unit. I started with my textbook, Tarbuck and Lutgens's *Earth Science* (2018). Figure 5.2 shows the objectives listed at the beginning of the chapter on volcanoes.

These objectives are pretty heavy on the lower levels of Bloom's taxonomy. Moreover, there are just too many of them—12, in fact. Note that objectives generally combine sections from the textbook. I didn't address all the textbook sections because, if I covered everything, I would never finish a course. Therefore, I have condensed the objectives into the following five essential questions:

- What secrets lie beneath the volcano and provide clues to how it will erupt? (Lessons 6.1–6.2)
- How do volcanoes form, and how can they be classified? (Lessons 6.3–6.6)
- What determines whether volcanoes are deadly or not? (Lesson 6.7)
- Can volcanoes have a global effect on the Earth? (Lesson 6.7)
- How is the global distribution of volcanoes related to plate tectonics? (Lesson 6.8)

At this point, I'm going to fill in the mastery template with both my driving and essential questions (see Figure 5.3). Please do the same now with your unit.

Figure 5.2 Chapter Objectives from an Earth Science Textbook

1	Compare and contrast the 1980 eruption of Mount St. Helens with the most recent eruption of Kilauea, which began in 1983.
2	Explain why some volcanic eruptions are explosive and others are quiescent
3	List and describe the three categories of materials extruded during volcanic eruptions.
4	Draw and label a diagram that illustrates the basic features of a typical volcanic cone.
5	Summarize the characteristics of shield volcanoes and provide one example of this type of volcano.
6	Describe the formation, size, and composition of a cinder cone volcano.
7	List the characteristics of composite volcanoes and describe how they form.
8	Describe the major geologic hazards associated with volcanoes.
9	List volcanic landforms other than shield, cinder cone, and composite volcanoes and describe their formation.
10	Compare and contrast these intrusive igneous structures: dikes, sills, batholiths, stocks, and laccoliths.
11	Summarize the major processes that generate magma from solid rock.
12	Explain how the global distribution of volcanic activity is related to plate tectonics.

Source: Adapted from *Earth Science*, by E. J. Tarbuck and F. K. Lutgens, 2018, Pearson.

Figure 5.3 Jon's In-Progress Mastery Plan with Driving and Essential Questions

Driving Question(s)

> *What are the types, causes, and effects of volcanic activity on Earth?*

Clear Unit Objectives/Essential Questions

> • What secrets lie beneath the volcano and provide clues to how it will erupt? (Lessons 6.1–6.2)
> • How do volcanoes form, and how can they be classified? (Lesson 6.3–6.6)
> • What determines whether volcanoes are deadly or not? (Lesson 6.7)
> • Can volcanoes have a global effect on the Earth? (Lesson 6.7)
> • How is the global distribution of volcanoes related to plate tectonics? (Lesson 6.8)

Creating the Mastery Rubric

Once you have established your clear learning objectives, it's time to move on to creating a mastery rubric. Figure 5.4 offers a blank copy you can work with.

Figure 5.4 Mastery Rubric Template

Lesson	Proof of Basic Understanding "I sort of get it."	Proof of Clear Understanding "I get it."	Proof of Deeper Understanding "I really get it."
1			
2			
...			

Summative Assessment Plan

Pre-test Plan

Lesson Planning

Lesson	Lesson Objective	Independent-Space Objects	Group-Space Objects	Formative Assessment Tools
1				
2				
...				

Remediation Plan

The mastery rubric was first developed by Andrew Swan, the middle school history teacher I mentioned earlier. Andrew calls the rubric a *mission tracker*. He uses elements of gamification in his class and finds that such terminology makes things more engaging for students. I use gamification as well, so my students also refer to the mastery rubric as the mission tracker. Figure 5.5 shows one of Andrew's mission trackers.

Figure 5.5 Andrew Swan's Mastery Rubric

What Is Government? Who Needs It?!

YOUR MISSIONS	Proof of Basic Understanding "You sort of get it."	Proof of Clear Understanding "You get it!"	Proof of Deeper Understanding "You totally get it!"
1. I can explain why all communities have some form of government.	• List three ways that a government can help a community. AND • Understand the meaning of these "Need2Know terms": constitution, autocracy, republic, direct democracy, rule of law, and common good/welfare.	• Explain why all communities need some form of government (include at least three "Need2Know terms"). AND • Reflect on why your section's class constitution will or won't be successful (provide at least two clear reasons).	• Reflect on why your section's class constitution will or won't be successful (provide two clear reasons and include supporting details from at least one class activity and at least one historical example).
2. I can analyze the concept of a social contract.	• Define "social contract" in your own words, with an original example from real life. AND • Identify three different philosophers' ideas about the best form of government.	• Explain the major differences among three philosophers' ideas about natural rights and human nature. OR • Create a dialogue among three characters that explains the major differences among three philosophical ideas about natural rights and human nature.	• Make a personal judgment about which is the best form of government or social contract. AND • Provide at least two reasons why you think so (include supporting details from at least one class activity and at least one historical example).
3. I can summarize the messages of the Declaration of Independence.	• List the topics of all five parts of the Declaration of Independence. AND • Compare the Declaration's structure to another document.	• Make a "Handy Declaration" (https://tinyurl.com/HandyDeclaration) with original and appropriate labels for all parts. AND • Reflect on the message of the Declaration's second part in the Mission 3 Reflection form at https://tinyurl.com/missionthreereflection.	• Write a Declaration of Independence with the same structure and messages as the original document from a different, assigned perspective (e.g., the perspective of John Hancock or Abigail Adams).

Essentially, Andrew has placed three clear objectives in the first column, under "Your Missions," and then defined what mastery looks like at each of three levels. In the "I get it" columns, he chooses action verbs for each checkbox item. Most of the checkboxes allow for a variety of choices as to how students will demonstrate mastery. For example, students might choose written responses, posters, videos, discussions, or recorded ways of demonstrating mastery. He doesn't much care *how* students demonstrate mastery; He just cares *that* they demonstrate it.

There are several reasons for building choice into mastery tasks. Andrew shared that some students write their responses and then finish explaining their ideas to him orally because their written output was slow (or because it's a way to meet the extra time accommodation of students with an individualized learning plan). For others, he accepts a written outline of their ideas without requiring the students to write full paragraphs. He does this to accommodate different levels of ability in his classes.

So, getting back into my head, how will I convert my volcano essential questions into a mastery rubric? To create these activities, I searched science standards on the internet, used my own expertise, and looked at past lessons and activities I knew were successful. Figure 5.6 shows what I came up with.

Creating the volcano unit rubric took me about 45 minutes of looking at the essential questions, considering the authentic tasks suggested in my state standards, perusing activities I had previously used, and searching the textbook for application and analysis activities and questions. This is a work in progress. As I use this rubric in the classroom, I will continue to modify and tweak it over the course of several years.

Of course, now it's time for you to put this book down and develop your own mastery rubric. If you don't know what mastery looks like for your class, how will you know what your students actually know? To help you create your mastery rubric, you can access a variety of completed mastery learning plans at TheMasteryLearningHandbook.com. These plans reflect a wide variety of disciplines and class levels and should provide some solid guidance.

Figure 5.6 Mastery Rubric (Mission Tracker) for Jon's Volcano Unit

Lesson	Lesson Objective	Proof of Basic Understanding "I sort of get it."	Proof of Clear Understanding "I get it."	Proof of Deeper Understanding "I really get it."
6.1–6.2	What secrets lie beneath the volcano and provide clues to how it will erupt?	• Explain the causes of the Mount St. Helens eruption. AND • Explain how the viscosity of magma helps identify how the volcano will erupt.	• Compare and contrast the silica content, viscosity, and explosiveness of the different types of magma. AND • Infer the most important component of magma in determining the explosiveness of a volcanic eruption.	• Design an experiment that models the viscosity flow of a volcano and illustrates how it erupts. OR • Model the effect of trapped gases on the explosiveness of magma and the behavior of solid particles in magma using raisins, vinegar, and baking soda.
6.3–6.6	How do volcanoes form, and how can they be classified?	• Sketch the three main types of volcanoes and explain how each forms. AND • Explain how the type of volcano determines how it will erupt. AND • Give at least two examples of each of the three main types of volcanoes.	• Explain how the type of magma is related to the type of eruption that will occur. AND • Explain how the slope of a volcano is indicative of the type of igneous rock from which it was made.	• Connect Bowen's reaction series to the type of volcano formed. OR • Choose one volcano. Explain its unique geology and what caused it to form or erupt in the way it did.

(continued)

Figure 5.6 Mastery Rubric (Mission Tracker) for Jon's Volcano Unit —(*continued*)

Lesson	Lesson Objective	Proof of Basic Understanding "I sort of get it."	Proof of Clear Understanding "I get it."	Proof of Deeper Understanding "I really get it."
6.7	What determines whether volcanoes are deadly or not? Can volcanoes have a global effect on the Earth?	• List the eight types of hazards posed by volcanoes. AND • List at least four effects volcanoes have on the entire Earth. AND • Explain the Volcanic Explosivity Index (VEI) and contrast three different volcanic eruptions.	• Explain the eight different hazards of volcanoes. Select the one you believe is the most damaging. Support your choice with evidence. AND • Choose the hazard that you think is least damaging Support your ideas in a three- to four-paragraph essay.	• Write a first-person narrative of someone who lived through a major eruption. OR • Create a video that describes what you believe is the greatest threat that volcanoes pose to the world. Support your choice with evidence. OR • Write a short narrative describing what it would be like if the Yellowstone supervolcano were to erupt.
6.8	How is the global distribution of volcanoes related to plate tectonics?	• Sketch the ring of fire and discuss how this relates to how some volcanoes form. AND • Identify global patterns of earthquake and volcanic activity.	• Contrast a hotspot volcano with a subduction zone volcano and explain their respective origins.	• Create a simulation that shows how a hotspot volcano can create a series of volcanoes over millions of years.

6

Planning Your Mastery Assessments

The next step in developing your mastery learning plan is to develop your assessment plan. If you look again at the mastery learning cycle (see p. 35), you will note that assessment appears twice: You plan the assessments first, then students complete them during the unit and toward its end. Because we're following backward design (where we start with the end in mind), planning assessments is the next step.

The big question to ask when thinking about assessment is this: *How will you know if students have mastered your curriculum?*

Does someone who is embarking on mastery learning need to create all-new assessments? My answer is no. Changing the way you assess students on top of everything else is a big ask, so if you don't make that change in the first year or two of mastery learning, that's fine. When I first made the jump, I used the same tests I had always given; I didn't change any of them! It wasn't until year two or three that I began to rethink assessments. Most teachers who make the move into mastery learning eventually do.

Even if you plan to put this step on hold for a while, I encourage you not to skip this chapter, as it describes some valuable skills that make assessment more manageable. Go ahead and highlight areas of interest and note some changes you might consider making in Year 2 or Year 3.

One of the crucial elements in mastery learning is that students need to master content *before* moving on to the next topic. You will need to provide a way for students who have not shown mastery on their first attempt to show mastery on a subsequent assessment. But first, let's look at the question of summative assessments.

Summative Assessments: To Give or Not to Give?

It was interesting to listen to the mastery learning experts I interviewed for this book as they discussed their approaches to assessment. Some gave large end-of-unit and end-of-course summative assessments, whereas others didn't do any summative assessments. Most of those who gave high-stakes assessments were required to do so. Some believed that summative assessments better prepared students for advancement to subsequent levels in education, whereas others administered assessments after each lesson.

I give summative assessments because they push students to synthesize their learning. It just seems too easy for students to complete a task and then forget what they have learned. Thus, at the end of every learning cycle (which contains five to seven learning objectives/essential questions), my students must demonstrate mastery on a summative assessment. It's an arrangement that also supports formative assessment, because students will restudy and retest until they demonstrate mastery.

Start with the End in Mind

Early in my career, I took a class that focused on Steven Covey's now-updated book *The 7 Habits of Highly Effective People* (2020). That course changed my life. Habit 2 states, "Begin with the end in mind." This is backward design in a nutshell. When designing a mastery learning class, I encourage you to develop your assessments *before* you design the specific lessons. These include your pre-tests, formative assessments, and summative assessments. And don't just think in terms of traditional assessments, where students respond in writing to prompts. Authentic and nonstandard assessments offer endless possibilities and will cause many of you to think differently about assessments.

Before we go any further, take out your unit plan and start thinking about your summative assessments. What form will they take? Will they be a series of questions? Or will your summative assessment be a project of some kind? One school I work with interviews students verbally about their learning. Paper-and-pencil assessments still play an essential role in clarifying the status of students' progress, but they are augmented with other means of discovery, like these brief interviews. I often assign video projects for my students to complete. However you choose to assess your students, be sure those assessments align with your clear objectives or essential questions.

Here are some tips on designing summative assessments with mastery learning in mind:

- **Vary your summative assessments so they're not all traditional exams.** Just to clarify, I still use traditional assessments sometimes because sometimes they're the best tool, and I put my paper-and-pencil tests online to make it easier to manage grading. But I also allow students to complete projects for summative assessments. If students can find some alternative way to effectively demonstrate their mastery of the content, they have my permission to do so.
- **Target your assessment questions.** I admit that I've not always done this the way I should. My computerized system draws on huge question banks, and to populate those banks, I search the internet for quality questions. But many of the questions don't actually assess what I have taught, and they have confused my students. I'm now in Year 3 of implementing mastery after an eight-year break from teaching full time, and I'm seeing that my process of creating quality assessment questions is improving each year.
- **Weave in questions from previous units.** Research shows that it's best to add questions and prompts from previous units to summative assessments (see Guskey, 2010). This practice places knowledge in long-term memory and helps students solidify learning.
- **Use more than just multiple-choice or recall questions.** Make sure your questions dive deeper into the content. Ask long-answer questions or have students show their work to a math problem. The objective isn't just getting students to know a bunch of information; instead, we want them to be able to use it, analyze it, and synthesize it.
- **In place of traditional exams, have students ask questions.** Finnish author, teacher, and researcher Marika Toivola sometimes has students just write out questions as their summative assessment. The quality of student questions is a window into their understanding of a topic. After they have submitted the questions, Marika follows up with a conversation where she digs a little deeper into their level of mastery. For example, when a student asks a shallow, surface-level question, it might indicate a lack of preparation, an incomplete understanding, or a low level of engagement. Deeper and complicated questions reveal a more nuanced understanding and testify to effective instruction. Often, the teachers

leading these discussions find the questions advance everyone's learning. I recall an exchange student from China who asked very insightful questions about earthquakes. Having lived through several, he had a keen interest and background knowledge on the topic and was able to share with the whole class some of his insights and related research.

- **Create alternate assessments.** Several of my summative assessments evaluate a student's knowledge through a hands-on activity. Just recently, my physics students had to drop a ball over a moving toy car and have it land in the cup on the top of the car. They had two chances to hit the target; if they failed on the first attempt, I required them to get some corrective feedback on their math before trying again. This activity covered all that we had learned in the unit, and it represented a sizable percentage of the students' summative assessment score.

Creating Summative Assessments

My go-to assessments are generated through our learning management system. (For more guidance on how to create multiple versions of summative assessments, see Chapter 11.) When students sit down to take a summative assessment, they are randomly assigned a series of questions that address each major objective of a unit. Students must score a minimum percentage (80 percent) to demonstrate mastery. If they do, they move on. If they don't, after some remedial work, they take a different assessment that pulls new questions from the same banks.

If students don't pass the summative assessment, should you allow them to move on to the next topic? This depends on your context and on what you teach. I usually allow students who have not passed to move on to the next topic so they don't get inextricably behind. However, I require these students to go back and demonstrate mastery on the need-to-know topics in the previous unit. Having them continue on has helped with the logistics of making mastery learning work.

I learned early in this journey that developing and writing good assessments are not easy. It can be helpful to investigate other sources of questions and add them to your repertoire. Science teacher Bob Furlong uses Problem-Attic.com with great success. It's a giant bank of questions organized by subject and standards. This gives Bob a greater range of questions to ask in his summative assessments.

But don't limit yourself to question banks. Be willing to assign authentic assessments, such as projects or interviews. PBLworks.org offers a good source of project-based learning (PBL) assessments. They have a project designer feature—an online, interactive planning tool that includes a library of 73 standards-based PBL projects that helps you design age-appropriate projects organized by and tied to most school standards (see www.pblworks.org/pbl-resources/project-designer).

Summative Assessments: To Retake or Not to Retake?

When chatting with the mastery experts, I was surprised that some of them didn't permit students to retake summative assessments. Gilbert Fong, an economics professor in Singapore, only allows retakes on formative assessments. His students can only take his summative exams once.

Science teacher Bob Furlong also gives only one summative assessment. However, he expects that students will correct all mistakes once they get the tests back. Teachers Corey Sullivan and Tim Kelly, on the other hand, allow for retakes. Their students must score a minimum of 70 percent on every summative assessment to pass and move on. With retakes, the teachers find that 99 percent of their students ultimately pass every exam.

The vast majority of teachers I spoke with allow students to retake summative assessments. Holly Stuart, an 8th grade science teacher in South Carolina, offers short summative assessments. Once students finish a mastery learning cycle, they take a 10-question quiz, and if they score greater than 70 percent, they move on to the next level. Megan Pierce, a high school physics and chemistry teacher, does her summative exams on Schoology, her school's learning management system, and she allows students to take them as many times as they need to score at least 70 percent.

My system is similar in that I, too, use my learning management system to deliver summative assessments. I also allow students to take their summative assessments as many times as they need to score at least 80 percent. I do, however, have a rule: If a student is unsuccessful, I expect them to get help before they retake the assessment. They can also take only one summative assessment each day.

I encourage you to allow for retakes. Remember, we don't care *when* students master material, only that they do, in fact, master it.

Finnish teacher Marika Toivola shared some refreshing views about retakes. She noted that most of her students initially saw any kind of failure as a negative. But because students can retake tests in her engineering and mathematics classes, they now celebrate failure as just another step in the learning journey. Marika does acknowledge that it takes a bit of time to convince students that failure is good for them. The key, she says, is to build a culture in your classroom that fosters collaboration so all students see that the goal of the class isn't to get a high grade but, rather, simply to learn. So, in one sense, all assessments, even summative assessments, are formative.

Tying Your Summative Assessment to the Mastery Rubric

One of the most transformative phone calls I had while researching this book was with Marika Toivola. In her book *Flipped Assessment: A Leap Towards Assessment for Learning* (2020), she questions the value of using one summative assessment at the end of a unit. Marika believes that the goal of any assessment is to discover at what level students comprehend a topic. To that end, she designs her assessments so that students reach a point of failure. She creates three separate assessments for each chapter or unit—one that demonstrates basic understanding, one that demonstrates clear understanding, and one that demonstrates deeper understanding. This notion fits perfectly with the mastery rubric and with the three levels of mastery students can demonstrate.

The reason this call was so transformative is that I have struggled with my one-size-fits-all mastery assessments. Last year, every student of mine passed every mastery assessment. But I'm also aware that I didn't always include the most challenging questions in every assessment. Marika showed me how to summatively determine at what level students have mastered the material—with basic, clear, or deeper understanding. Students get to choose which test they take—and they can take all three of them if they wish—with their grade depending on the highest level of the test they pass (see Chapter 15 for details). Going forward, I will have three different tests for each unit.

Developing Your Summative Assessment Plan

Now it's time for you to put down this book and develop your own summative assessment plan. Pull out your Mastery Unit Planning Template and, in the space indicated, describe the assessment you'll be using, whether it's a traditional or nonstandard assessment. You need to write this down first *before* developing lessons.

I'm going to do this right along with you. Again, I'm working on my volcano unit. Figure 6.1 shows my summative assessment plan.

Figure 6.1 Summative Assessment Plan for Jon's Volcano Unit

- Students will choose to take one or more of three different summative assessments—for *basic, clear,* or *deeper* understanding. The highest level they pass determines their grade.
- Students must score a minimum of 80 percent on whichever test they choose.
- If students choose the deeper understanding assessment, they must complete a five-minute interview with me in which I check for true deeper understanding. The focus of that conversation will be the question *What are the types, causes, and effects of volcanic activity on the Earth?*

Diagnostic Pre-Assessment

In his book *Educational Psychology*, American psychologist David Ausubel (1968) wrote, "If I had to reduce all of educational psychology to just one principle, I would say this: The most important single factor influencing learning is what the learner already knows. Ascertain this and teach him accordingly" (p. vi).

Does that mean that in the mastery cycle we should pre-assess students just after we create our assessments and before we engage in lesson planning? Benjamin Bloom was not a big fan of pre-testing in a mastery class. He worried that most of the time, students would start out with failure. In addition, he believed that the prerequisite for the subsequent topic in a given subject was mastery of the previous content.

Another flag that's been raised about pre-testing is some teachers' practice of grading students in terms of improvement—how far they have come over the course of the unit. The argument goes that students who are wise to this could purposely score low on the pre-assessment to inflate their grade when they take the post-assessment.

In light of these potential pitfalls, is there a place for pre-assessment? Felipe Leyton Soto (1983), a student of Benjamin Bloom, argued that if prerequisite knowledge is necessary to complete a lesson, a short pre-test followed by correctives will significantly improve student outcomes. This may be especially important if you're teaching students who have gaps in their learning caused by the recent pandemic.

Someone who does pre-testing well is Steve Crapnell, a math teacher and the head of digital pedagogy at All Hallows' School in Brisbane, Australia. He uses pre-tests to determine if students have all the prerequisite background knowledge they need to complete lessons. Because Steve teaches math, much of what students will learn in his class depends on prior knowledge. So, if students don't know how to do X, then Y is even harder. Figure 6.2 shows a series of questions Steve includes on a pre-test for his calculus class. Note that right next to the questions are original videos he's made to help students who don't get it. He has built the correctives right into the process.

When should you pre-assess? If you see the potential for gaps in prerequisite knowledge, do a pre-assessment. For me, I look at this on a lesson-by-lesson basis. Last year, I saw the need for more pre-assessments, especially in math skills, in both my physics and chemistry classes. Some students didn't have the necessary math background, and I needed to create correctives for them.

So let's go back to your Mastery Unit Planning Template, which we looked at in Chapter 4 (see p. 37). If you need to pre-test, add it to your plan in the space provided. I'm going to leave this section blank because I don't see the need to pre-test students in this unit on volcanoes.

Figure 6.2 Steve Crapnell's Trigonometry Pre-Test: A Sample

Content	Video Resource
Question 1 Determine the exact value of the following: (i) sin 60 (ii) tan $\frac{3\pi}{4}$ (iii) cos $\frac{5\pi}{3}$	FL 3.5 Exact Ratios FL 3.6 Angles in Four Quadrants
Question 2 Determine all solutions for each of the following: (i) sin $x \frac{\sqrt{3}}{2}$ $0 \leq x \leq 2\pi$ (ii) 2 cos $x + 1 = 0$ [0, 360] (iii) 2 − 5 cos + 1 = 0 [0, 360]	FL 3.10 Solutions to Trig Equations 1 FL 3.11 Solutions to Trig Equations 2

7

Creating Tools for Formative Assessment

We have now arrived at the lesson planning stage of the mastery learning cycle. Lesson planning has four main components: formative assessment, independent-space learning objects, group-space learning objects, and reflection (see Figure 7.1). We will consider each of these four components in this chapter and the three chapters that follow.

Like me, some of you might want to create the learning objects *before* developing the formative assessment tools. It doesn't matter which you choose. If you want to go that route, read Chapters 8 and 9 now and then return to Chapter 7 afterward.

Figure 7.1 Components of an Effective Mastery Lesson Plan

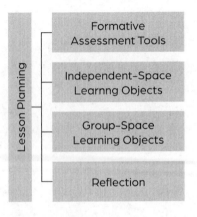

Formative Assessment: Mastery Checks

The heart of mastery learning is not in the summative assessment at the end of units but in the formative checks for understanding and progress conducted throughout the unit. For mastery learning to work, you need lots of low-stakes assessments that provide in-the-moment feedback to both teachers and students. Most flipped-mastery teachers have adopted the term *mastery check* to describe this process.

Mastery checks can take many forms. Let's explore a few of the types that teachers are using to inform their instructional decisions.

Student-taught content

Lisa McCauley, a 7th grade math teacher in Illinois, walks around her classroom with a whiteboard. When students give her a sign that they're ready for a mastery check, she gives them the whiteboard and asks them to explain to the class what they've learned about the day's topic. We all know that we learn best when we have to explain something to someone else, so this idea is brilliant.

During these sessions, Lisa sometimes steps in if a student is struggling; other times, she holds back, confident that the student will eventually come around to understanding. According to Lisa, "The art is knowing when to help and when to just listen."

Paper assessments

Hannah Curran, a 3rd grade teacher in Illinois, uses what she calls *interview assessments*. When students are ready to get checked for mastery, she plops down a short problem they need to solve. (She uses this approach during math instruction, but she's also found it useful in reading and writing lessons.) Once students have solved the problem, they must explain to her how they solved it and why they chose to address it that way. If you're going to use this approach, you will need to create a bank of questions to assess student learning.

I intend to use these short interview assessments in my classes next year. This will be especially useful in my chemistry and physics classes, because those classes are quite math-centric. You can also use these short assessments to target skills you want students to demonstrate. For example, if your goal is for students to identify all the similes in a passage, have students complete a short assessment right after the lesson that demonstrates their understanding. The possibilities are endless.

Online mastery checks

Ohio science teacher Bob Furlong uses his school's learning management system, Schoology, to support his formative assessment efforts. He creates three different mastery checks for each objective and writes the questions in such a way that the computer will grade them automatically. Students have three attempts to get it right; if they're unsuccessful on their third attempt, they are required to have a remediation sit-down with the teacher.

Student-led questioning

I learned early in my flipped-mastery journey to let students ask questions. Each student is expected to bring at least one good question for each lesson. I have found during these question times that getting inside my students' heads requires me to be quiet and listen. These questions are a powerful insight into student comprehension of a topic. Sometimes their questions reveal a misconception. A student once asked me why a certain number was in a chemical reaction, and I realized that they didn't understand the basics of how chemicals react (something they should have learned in the past). Other times, their questions are too surface-level, and students simply ask a question that is readily explained in the prework. When this occurs, I usually turn it back and ask them if they have watched the video or read the prework. And sometimes their questions take me deeper, and we explore cool stuff together. For example, a student recently asked how it is possible for an air conditioner to work since heat always flows from hot to cold. This deeper question showed a great understanding, and it led to a deep conversation about how we cool air.

Whiteboard assessments

Emma Parkinson, a Years 3–4 teacher (students are ages 6–8) at the Ashhurst Primary School in New Zealand, walks around her classroom with a portable whiteboard, quickly writing prompts that students are challenged to respond to on the spot. Especially in math, it's a fast way to check if students have mastered the important aspects of a topic.

Verbal assessments or microconversations

Heath Chittenden, principal of Ashhurst Primary School, notes that formative assessment is "all about the quality of the questions." Ashhurst, by the way, was the first flipped school in New Zealand. Heath encourages his staff to be clear about what they want students to know and be able to do and to factor this into the questions they ask students in their mastery checks. One form of mastery check is the *microconversation*, conducted individually or in small groups. Personally, I favor small groups of about four students because this arrangement enables student to learn from the reflections of their peers.

I have found that I need to have better key questions in hand for each mastery check. One or two essential questions always get to the heart of the specific learning that students are doing. I need to do a better job of writing these down on my clipboard so I can be ready to ask them.

Some have asked me how I know if a student has mastered a topic if all we're doing is talking. I have typically relied on my gut and on what the quality of the conversation with the student tells me. This aspect of my teaching is more art than science. If the student's comments reveal deep understanding, the student has mastered the topic. This method is most successful in my geology class, which is highly descriptive, as opposed to in my physics and chemistry classes, where students must solve discrete problems. In geology, students need to explain to me the causes of thunder or earthquakes or why it's almost always cold in Alaska. If they can explain a phenomenon adequately, then I check the box that indicates that they have mastered it. This method also works well in a literature class where you want students to explain why a certain character acted the way he or she did or what the main theme of a poem is.

Frankly, these microconversations may be the biggest source of joy in my teaching career. To walk around my classroom and hear the quality of student thinking, to be able to push the students to go deeper and learn more and to challenge them—it just doesn't get any better than this.

Good questions, amazing consequences

When I used to teach in a more traditional manner, I would lecture about a specific topic at a given time during the year, asking the relevant questions during that one segment. But things have changed since I began to teach with mastery learning. Because the conversations during mastery checks aren't taking place in front of the whole class but are held individually or in small groups, I have these conversations with students far more often now. As a result, I've had a lot more practice asking better questions.

I even craft the questions differently for different students. For some students, my class is quite challenging, and I want them to have a more general understanding of the material. For others, the class is in their wheelhouse, and

I take them deeper, so we end up learning so much more than the published course objectives.

Technology Tools That Enhance Formative Assessment

Choosing a platform for your assessments can be daunting. When I returned to teaching full time, I scoured the internet for a learning management system that had a robust assessment tool. I eventually landed on Brightspace, from the Canadian company D2L. It has served me well. That said, all technology tools have some limitations.

The host of experts I interviewed for this book use a variety of tools to do mastery assessments, which shows that there's no one right tool. Here are some of the tools they suggest:

- MasteryConnect.com
- Microsoft 365 Suite
- Problem-Attic.com
- Schoology
- Seesaw
- Google Classroom and Google Forms

You can find another category of assessment suites with most curriculum publishers. If your teaching is closely aligned with your textbook, the publisher is likely to have a comprehensive assessment suite that mirrors what you teach. I'm quite impressed with SAS, a Brazilian publisher (see https://saseducacao.com.br/). In their assessment suite, not only do they have a huge bank of questions, but they have also added elements of artificial intelligence and gamification that enhance student learning. One of their products gets students prepared for the equivalent of the Brazilian SAT, and that tool has shown huge improvements in student success.

Mastery teachers are using Canvas (www.instructure.com/canvas), Blackboard (www.blackboard.com), Nearpod (https://nearpod.com), Mentimeter (www.mentimeter.com), and a whole host of other tools. Some tools are better for summative assessment, whereas others are better for formative assessment. And don't forget the value of paper-and-pencil assessments. The ability for students to quickly show their work often makes these the simplest tool for gaining insight into their evolving understanding.

Last, I acknowledge that, in many cases, the software tool you have available may have been predetermined by others. If this is the case, try to make do with it and be sure to learn all its ins and outs.

Adding Your Formative Assessment Instruments to Your Plan

I now will add my formative assessment instruments to my volcano unit, which in my case involves using a simple interview/microconversation methodology. In other lessons, I will use other methods that we have discussed.

Go ahead and do this planning work now.

8

Creating Independent-Space Learning Objects

With formative assessment plans set, it's time to add in the activities that you will have students complete in class. In this chapter, we'll look at creating independent-space learning objects.

You might wonder about the term *learning objects*. Polsani (2003) surveyed various definitions in use and settled on this: "A learning object is an independent and self-standing unit of learning content that is predisposed to reuse in multiple instructional contexts" (para. 22). Although this definition covers a lot of what might happen in class, including a presentation of new information, practice items, assessment items, and so on—we will look specifically at independent- and group-space learning objects. (We'll discuss the former in this chapter and the latter in Chapter 9.) Once you have created these, you'll be nearly done with planning your first mastery learning unit.

What Are Independent-Space Learning Objects?

In independent space, students will, by and large, work alone. Here, students are introduced to new material; their learning is operating primarily in the lower two levels of Bloom's taxonomy—in the categories of remembering and understanding.

Most mastery learning teachers create or curate quality independent-space learning materials in one of two ways: they use either text-based or video prework. There are advantages and disadvantages to both. You probably have access to lots of text-based materials, so those might be easier to use initially as prework. And text-based materials are often more suitable for topics that are more complex and that contain significant nuance.

But video is often preferable—for example, when you're showing students how to do something (how to change an alternator for a mechanics class, how to solve a given problem in a math or physics class, how to cite a source, or how to identify conjunctions in a sentence). But, of course, creating video content requires more work from you, and all students need screens to access the content. Although designing and recording quality instructional videos will take some time and practice, you can perfect your video lectures as you become more accomplished in creating them. Most important, students can watch them as many times as they like, and they can pause and rewind them as needed.

So which should you use, text or video? One option is to give students a choice. Most of my videos mirror the sections in my textbook. For example, Section 6.2 in my geology textbook describes the different types of volcanoes. I created Video 6.2, which tackles the same topic. Students can either read Section 6.2 in the textbook or watch my video.

However, in some cases, I don't give students a choice. For example, in my physics class, I assign a textbook chapter about Michael Faraday, the person recognized as most responsible for discovering the various uses of electricity. The chapter recounts a moving story about how Faraday overcame tremendous obstacles to become one of the most outstanding scientists of all time. I am unaware of any video that is as powerful. So, choosing textual or video prework depends on the nature of the lesson. Figure 8.1 presents some points to keep in mind when deciding between the two.

Figure 8.1 Advantages and Disadvantages of Video and Text as Prework

Format	Advantages	Disadvantages
Video	• Best at showing how to do something • Best if a visual representation is paired with an explanation • Similar to a lecture and works as a lecture replacement	• Difficult to edit if the material becomes outdated • Harder to create • Requires a significant up-front time commitment if you're creating your own videos • Takes an inordinate amount of teacher time to search out the perfect video when using curated content
Text	• Easy to edit if the content becomes outdated • Helps make students better readers	• Not well suited for showing steps • Copyright may be an issue • Harder to make digital

Video Prework: Create or Curate?

A common question about using video as prework is this: *Do I need to create my own videos, or can I use materials that others have made?* This is an ongoing debate in the flipped-learning community.

When I started down the flipped-mastery path, I created all my own video content. Part of that was out of necessity. In 2007, there weren't many high-quality instructional videos online, and YouTube had barely been born. Today you can find a video on almost anything, and YouTube likely has a variety on every topic you teach. But they vary in quality, accuracy, and effectiveness.

When I returned to the classroom in 2019, I created brand-new videos. Relationships are the heart and soul of good teaching, and when my students see me in the video, it enhances the student-teacher relationship. In addition, it communicates to my students that I'm an expert in my subject. Having worked with thousands of flipped-learning teachers, I've found that classrooms just run smoother when teachers create their own videos. When teachers curate other content, students may go home thinking that their teacher simply "isn't teaching anymore." Creating your own content is a good way to combat this sentiment.

However, I'm not saying you need to create *all* your own content. I use other people's videos occasionally. Some people can explain a topic in a way that is far superior to my own. I tend to use other people's content when I'm teaching something I haven't totally mastered. For example, I recently did a unit on electromagnetic induction. The last time I taught that unit was 30 years ago. So I decided to watch some YouTube videos to brush up on my knowledge of the topic so I could do a better job of teaching it. Then I just decided to use the videos I was learning from and assign those to my students. That said, next year I will create my own videos on electromagnetic induction.

A teacher in a workshop I was leading articulated another reason to create your own videos. He said, "I could spend hours and hours looking for the perfect YouTube video, or I could just make it myself." You may have a certain way you teach a specific topic; trying to find a video that teaches the way you do will most likely take more time than just making it yourself. Once you have mastered some technical hurdles, creating your own instructional videos is not very difficult. And as you make more videos, you will find that it takes less time and the quality improves.

You may have already dipped your toes into video creation. Perhaps during the pandemic, with so much of schooling taking place remotely, you learned how to make short instructional videos. Maybe you used screen capture software, such as Screencast-O-Matic (www.screencast-o-matic.com) or Screencastify (www.screencastify.com).

If you're ready to refine the quality of your instructional videos, a number of research-based best practices can help.

Best Practices for Video Content

Adhering to the following best practices will up the quality of your videos and make them both more effective and more appealing to your students.

Highlight the objective

Be sure your videos communicate the essential questions or main objective of the lesson or unit. Right at the start of the video, tell students exactly what you want them to learn. I didn't do this in the past. This year, I went back and added text boxes to all my videos to highlight the objective.

Keep videos short

My first instructional videos were too long. I tried to cram all that I used to teach in one class period into a video. Effective videos teach *one topic at a time*. As for length, the general rule is that your videos shouldn't be any longer than the age of your students. If you teach 7-year-olds, keep your videos to 7 minutes; if you teach 10-year-olds, keep them to 10 minutes. I teach high school juniors and seniors who are 17 and 18 years old. My videos range from 7 to 11 minutes long. Truly, videos should never be more than 15 minutes long, even if you're a college professor. This past year, I violated this rule when creating a new unit of study. My videos pushed 20 minutes, and my students really struggled. I should have known better, but I was in a rush. I'll be going back and creating a new set of shorter videos for next year's students.

Use videos to introduce new content

Keep your videos focused on the lower levels of Bloom's taxonomy, on understanding and remembering. Save the hard stuff for the group space.

Ensure each video has more pictures than words

Many first-time video creators tend to have text-heavy screens that they talk over. But video is a *visual* medium. If the text is that important, students should probably be doing reading as prework instead. In your videos, use images to illustrate your point. For example, if you're making a video about child labor during the Industrial Revolution, include images that depict what working conditions were like for the children. Then talk over the pictures with some of your key points.

Build in interactivity

Video can be a passive medium, but that shouldn't be the case with instructional videos. It's crucial to find ways for students to interact with the video content even while working alone in the independent space. There are a wide variety of ways to build in interactivity. Let's look at several of them.

Graphic Organizers

Using graphic organizers as an instructional video aid is up for debate. In 2018, Vitanofa and Anwar studied 77 students in a flipped writing class. Half of the students used graphic organizers, and the other half simply took notes from the instructional videos. Vitanofa and Anwar found a significant increase in achievement for those in the group using the organizers. When I first saw the 2018 study, I started making graphic organizers for my classes. Figure 8.2 shows one I use in my geology class.

Reviewing this organizers, notice the following:

- Essential questions are front and center.
- I include pre-video questions. In 2017, Carpenter and Toftness found that students who answered pre-video questions performed 19 percent higher than the control group.
- Questions, diagrams, and charts organize the information.
- There is space for students to summarize the video.
- There is space for students to write down questions to ask during their mastery checks in class.

You might recognize the table-style templates I've incorporated as reflecting elements of the Cornell note-taking strategy. (Cornell-style notes have really worked well for my students.)

I'm beginning to move away from having my older students use graphic organizers as instructional video aids. Some students just fill in the blanks and aren't engaging deeply with the video content. My plan going forward is to spend more time teaching students how to interact with instructional videos by

Figure 8.2 A Graphic Organizer as an Instructional Video Aid

Video 6.2: Oozy or Explody?
Video Essential Questions
- What are the two main types of magma?
- What is the difference between effusive and explosive eruptions?
- What is meant by the term *viscosity*?
- How does the melting point of a specific type of magma influence the type of eruption?

Pre-Video Question: Describe what you think happens when a bomb explodes. Think about a contained space and what must happen.

React to the video of an "oozy" volcano. What did you see, and what are you curious about?

Identify the four types of volcanoes below.

What is the key factor in how each type of volcano is formed?

Define: *Viscosity*

Define: *Pyroclastic flow*

Fill out the table.

Composition	Gas Content	Eruptive Temperatures	Viscosity	Tendency to Form Pyroclastic Flow	Type of Volcano
Balsatic (mafic)					
Andesitic (intermediate)					
Felsic					

(continued)

Figure 8.2 A Graphic Organizer as an Instructional Video Aid—(*continued*)

Define: *Quiescent*

What factors affect viscosity? Complete the table.

Factor	How Affected
Temperature	
Composition	

Video Summary

Question to Ask in Class

using a more open Cornell note-taking strategy, and then I'll have them create their own graphic organizers. I'll still require students to answer a pre-video question, summarize the video in their own words, and write down interesting questions that arise from watching the video. Note that younger students may benefit from using graphic organizers in this way because they may not be ready to process information at a higher level.

Embedded Questions

Several video interaction tools exist that let you embed questions in instructional videos to track your students' comprehension. Currently, many teachers use Edpuzzle (https://edpuzzle.com), Formative (www.formative.com), Play-Posit (https://go.playposit.com), and, to some degree, their school's learning management system. Most learning management systems don't yet have a robust video interaction component, but this will likely change as time goes on.

Another feature of these tools is the ability to force the video to pause. For example, if you want your students to stop and solve a problem or underline some text, you can make the video pause at a given point; students must then click on a button before they can continue. This forced pause not only makes the viewing experience more interactive, it gives students time to process important concepts.

Social Learning

One problem with students working independently is that they're learning alone. Research (Bielaczyc, 2013) has shown that students learn better when learning socially. One way to make the independent space social is to use a social video platform. For example, with the tool Perusall (https://perusall.com), teachers can link online videos to the platform, and then students watch the videos asynchronously. They can pause the video and add their own comments, which peers can respond to. Perusall has the same features for text-based prework, so I use the tool for both.

Perusall also offers what it calls a *confusion report*—that is, an automatically generated report that summarizes general areas of confusion or areas where students have questions. In Figure 8.3, you'll find a confusion report from one of my classes. It shows keywords that students keep mentioning—such as *minerals* and *scale*—and lists comments that illustrate where they're confused. The circled letters are the initials of the students who are commenting. Students can comment in each video, and often, their classmates will jump in to provide clarification before I do.

Figure 8.3 Perusall Confusion Report

Confusion report for a 2.4a Video: The Amazing Property of Minerals X

Topic 1 (keywords: minerals, scale) Part: 1

(LT) I find it interesting how diamond is the hardest mineral on the Mohs scale. Since diamond is the strongest mineral on the Mohs scale, is it not possible for any other mineral to scratch the mineral diamond?

(PD) What would happen if you had a mineral that did not scratch but did not fall under any other section? Would you just classify it as a lower level in the Hardness Scale?

(PD) What would happen if you could not see the inside part? For instance, if the mineral was a darker color?

Topic 2 (keywords: differently, exactly)

(LT) I think that it is interesting how two minerals with the same chemical composition form differently on Earth. What is the name of that chemical? Also, why does the same chemical form differently on Earth?

(WK) What makes crystals different from each other? It seems like they have different chemical and physical properties, but if they have different chemical and physical properties, why do we still classify them all as crystals?

(JY) How exactly are they different? The definitions seem the same.

Tracking Students' Viewing Behaviors

All of the tools I've mentioned track student video viewing: how much time students spent on each video, if they watched one part of the video multiple times, the percentage of each video they watched, and how they performed on all the embedded questions. This is a treasure trove of information that teachers can use to determine just how well each student comprehends each video.

Figure 8.4 shows a sample of the teacher view in Edpuzzle. Notice how some students got 100 percent of the questions correct and others did not. A teacher can also click on each student's name and get more detailed information about their specific viewing habits.

The teacher view in Perusall presents a dashboard of student data, including how much time each student spent viewing the assignment (it can distinguish between active reading and viewing time and just having the window or video open); the number of annotations, comments, and upvotes each students made; and the number of comments and upvotes their comments received.

I can't emphasize enough how important it is to use a tracking tool. Holding students accountable for doing the prework is essential in a mastery classroom. When students know that *you* know if and how much they interacted with the prework, it ensures greater success in the mastery learning experience.

Figure 8.4 The Teacher View in Edpuzzle

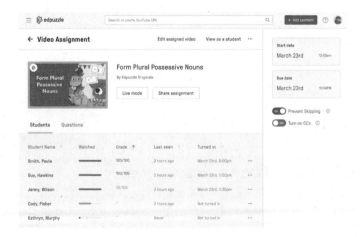

Best Practices for Video Creation

The content of a video is crucial. However, if you don't get the technology right, then all your content may be for naught. Here are a few tips to make sure your videos are top-notch from the point of view of technology.

Pay attention to audio quality

Nothing will ruin a good video like bad audio, and the single most important way to improve audio quality is to record in a quiet room. Another way is to put the microphone as close to your mouth as practicable. The built-in microphones on most devices are probably adequate for most instructional videos. If you need better-quality audio, I recommend buying a USB microphone or using a headset that connects to your computer.

Annotate

It's often beneficial to annotate your videos, providing another level of commentary to guide students toward the most important content. In my fields, chemistry and physics, annotation is essential. Here are some different ways to do it:

- **Record yourself at a whiteboard.** Put your smartphone on a tripod, stand at a whiteboard, and record yourself commenting on and annotating the text that's already written there.
- **Use touch-screen laptops.** Many laptops have touch screens, and these allow for easy writing. Purchase a digital pen to give you better control of your annotations.
- **Invest in an external pen tablet.** These devices are inexpensive and connect to a laptop through either USB or Bluetooth. I use a Wacom Intuos pen tablet.

Post videos online

You can often use learning management software to post directly to the platform. Some video interaction tools, such as Edpuzzle and PlayPosit, allow you to do the same with their platforms. You can also post your videos to services such as YouTube or Vimeo and then share the link with your students. Google Drive and Microsoft OneDrive also host videos.

Consider using a central access point

Many teachers simply create one Google Document that they share with their students. That document is the master document, and it has links to all of the class resources, such as online assignments, flipped videos, assessments, and so on. Ashhurst Primary School in New Zealand runs everything through Google Classroom and Google Docs with great success.

Partner with another teacher

Creating instructional videos is better done in teams. If you have a colleague with whom you can work, your video's quality and effectiveness will improve. Not only will the video be easier to create, but seeing two people in conversation on a screen is far more interesting than watching one person standing there lecturing. If you listen to the radio during your daily commute, two people are usually having a conversation; it isn't just one person trying to hold the audience's attention. It's an arrangement that increases interactivity and has the following positive effects:

- **Good ideas rise to the top.** Before you create the video, you will almost always have a conversation about the best way to teach a topic. That conversation is a built-in way to improve your teaching.
- **Different perspectives allow for more effective learning experiences.** Having a second person in the conversation on screen allows one of them to take the part of the teacher and the other to take the part of an inquisitive student who asks questions. Those questions are often key to understanding. For example, I once worked with a history teacher who was teaching about how the U.S. Supreme Court addressed racism in the early 1900s. As a science teacher, I was unfamiliar with the history, and I was indeed an inquisitive student. I learned a lot, and the teacher demonstrated his expertise in his field.
- **It reduces the workload.** In a pairs arrangement, one teacher might plan the videos, and the other might take care of some of the technological burdens.
- **It helps demonstrate mastery learning's value.** Working in pairs can be a catalyst for getting other teachers to try mastery learning. If you volunteer to help another teacher create videos, you may help them make

the jump to mastery learning. When I was a technology director, I helped many teachers create their first flipped videos. I assisted with the technological aspects, and I sat in as the inquisitive student. I'm currently working with another teacher who also teaches chemistry. We make our videos together, and although he has not yet fully embraced mastery learning, he's moving in that direction.

Speak naturally

When teachers make their first videos, they often lose some of the energy and enthusiasm they have when in front of a live audience. There *is* something weird about sitting at a computer screen and getting animated and energetic when nobody is there to see. The key is to know that an audience will be watching your video and will appreciate you bringing your best to your video.

This advice is supported by Richard Mayer's (2021) research in the field of multimedia design. He developed 12 principles, one of which is the Personalization Principle, which states that people learn better from multimedia lessons when words are in a conversational style rather than a formal style. Mayer suggests that the learner should feel like someone is talking directly to them when they hear your narration.

So be yourself. If you're quirky, be quirky. If you have a dry sense of humor, use it. If you're low-key, use your soothing voice to invite students to learn. And remember, when your students know that you're making these videos for them, it will mean something to them, and they will learn better.

Let students control the pace

Another of Mayer's principles is the Learner Control Principle—the idea that students experience deeper learning when they control the rate at which they move through segmented content (Scheiter, 2014). Learners do better if the video stops after short meaningful segments and they have to click to continue the video. Forcing learners to pause increases their comprehension.

A lot of software tools, such as Edpuzzle, allow you to insert pauses in videos. For example, Figure 8.5 (see p. 74) shows a still of a video at the point where I inserted a pause to ask a question. Pauses like these allow students to process what they have just seen and heard, and they must actively push a "Submit" button to proceed.

Figure 8.5 Video Pause in Edpuzzle

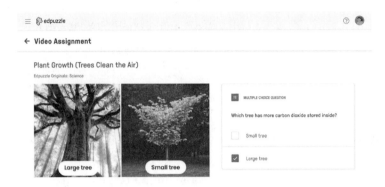

Text-Based Prework

Many flipped and mastery teachers use text-based assignments as independent-space learning objects. As with video, text-based prework must be done at the lower levels of Bloom's taxonomy (understanding and remembering). Students should be able to do this work independently.

Here are some of the advantages of using text-based prework:

- It's easily edited if you're planning to use the content in subsequent terms or years.
- It can address topics in a more profound manner.
- It encourages students to be readers.
- It requires more complex thinking.
- It takes less time to prepare than videos.
- It allows for more content (video transcripts tend to be short).

Harvard physics professor Eric Mazur flips his classes but doesn't use video. He finds that text-based prework is ideal for his style. I had a chance to visit Harvard Medical School, which has wholly flipped its learning, and most of their prework is also text-based. In my classes, I use a mix of video and text as prework.

You probably won't create a lot of text-based prework. Instead, you will curate it from a wide variety of sources. You can assign passages from a textbook, articles found online, anthologies, short stories, research articles, primary source documents, and a whole host of other sources.

One of the beauties of text-based prework is that it potentially requires no technology except for a book or a few sheets of paper. Depending on your context, this may be the best solution for your prework. However, if your students have adequate access to technology, you might want to consider delivering the text using *text interaction tools*. These tools track student reading time, provide opportunities for formative feedback, and make the learning social.

The Perusall video interaction tool I mentioned earlier was initially designed as a text-interaction tool, so it works even better in text mode. When students read the shared text, they can highlight, comment, and comment on other students' comments. The tool also assesses student comments and generates a confusion report, just as the video aspect of the tool does.

Figure 8.6 shows an excerpt of an interactive conversation linked to a text explanation of electrical charge. "JB" is me.

Figure 8.6 Sample Perusall Reading Interaction

IM: Are gravitational and electric fields mutually exclusive? Presumably objects that have electric fields are also massive and thus must have a gravitational field. Do the electric and magnetic fields interact at all?

JB: Gravitational and electric fields are not mutually exclusive. It is possible to have things that are both massive (and therefore exert a large gravitational field) and have a lot of charge (and therefore exert a large electric field). Electric and magnetic fields definitely interact! The interaction between these fields is behind a lot of technologies—radio, telegraph, and electromagnetic motors, to name just a few.

TY: We underestimate the impact of magnetic and electrostatic forces based on our familiarity with gravitational forces. For example, the g in gravity is much smaller than the K in electrostatic force. However, we have to remember that the Coulomb's constant K is so much greater because gravitational forces are much, much weaker than electrostatic forces. For example, rubbing a balloon against your hair creates a lot of electrostatic force but virtually no gravitational force.

Actively Learn (www.activelylearn.com) is another text interaction tool with valuable features. Kevin Sivils, a history teacher at my school, uses this with excellent results. He reports that his students are now actually reading the assigned text. Because the tool tracks student engagement and the time that students have spent reading the document—and students are aware that the teacher is reviewing those elements—student comprehension has vastly improved.

The screenshot in Figure 8.7 shows a reading I assigned to students using Actively Learn in the aftermath of Hurricane Harvey, which struck our region in August 2017. The vast majority of my students experienced this event. As you can see, there's a place where teachers can jot down notes and embed questions in the text.

Figure 8.7 Sample of the Actively Learn Text Interaction Tool

HOUSTON—Lightning crashed all around as I dashed into the dark night. The parking lot outside my apartment building had become swollen with rains, a torrent about a foot deep rushing toward lower ground God knows where. Amazingly, the garage door rose when I punched the button on the opener. Inside I found what I expected to find—mayhem.

In dismay, I scooped up a box of books that had been on the floor. As I did, one of the sodden bottom flaps gave way, and a heavy book splashed into the water. *From Dawn to Decadence,* a timeless account of the Western world's great works, by Jacques Barzun. Almost immediately, a current from the rushing water beyond the garage door pulled the tome away, forever. *Damn, I loved that book.* An indescribably bad night had just gotten a little bit worse.

MR. BERGMANN

This piece was written by Eric Berger, a Houston-based space guru.

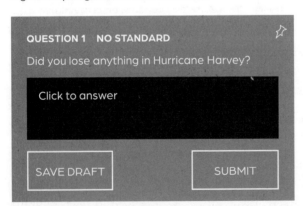

The student data view (see Figure 8.8) gives you a wealth of data, including how much time each student spent reading and which embedded questions they answered correctly.

Figure 8.8 Student Data View from Actively Learn

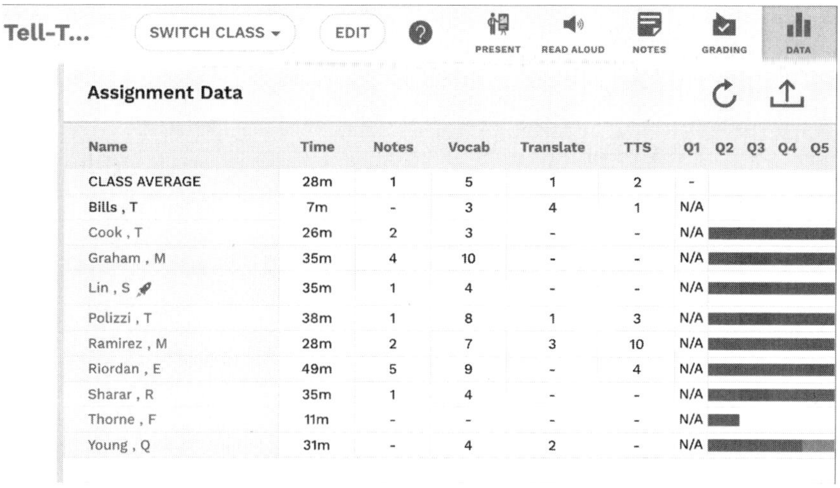

Name	Time	Notes	Vocab	Translate	TTS	Q1	Q2 Q3 Q4 Q5
CLASS AVERAGE	28m	1	5	1	2	-	
Bills, T	7m	-	3	4	1	N/A	
Cook, T	26m	2	3	-	-	N/A	
Graham, M	35m	4	10	-	-	N/A	
Lin, S	35m	1	4	-	-	N/A	
Polizzi, T	38m	1	8	1	3	N/A	
Ramirez, M	28m	2	7	3	10	N/A	
Riordan, E	49m	5	9	-	4	N/A	
Sharar, R	35m	1	4	-	-	N/A	
Thorne, F	11m	-	-	-	-	N/A	
Young, Q	31m	-	4	2	-	N/A	

Adding Independent-Space Learning Objects to the Mastery Unit Plan

To illustrate adding learning objects to the plan, I will continue to build my unit on volcanoes. Figure 8.9 (see p. 78) shows my entries for each learning objective. You need to think about each essential question and how you can best introduce students to the material. Will you choose a video, a text, or both? Remember to keep whatever you choose in the lower levels of Bloom's taxonomy.

You can see that students can choose either video or text prework. I also created graphic organizers for each video. Note that all videos and text are posted to Perusall for student interaction and that students must make at least four comments in each video or reading section.

I want you to get out your mastery learning plan and add your independent-space learning activities. Do that now.

Figure 8.9 Jon's Volcano Unit with Independent-Space Objects

Lesson	Lesson Objective	Independent-Space Objects	Group-Space Objects	Formative Assessment Tools
6.1–6.2	What secrets lie beneath the volcano and provide clues to how it will erupt?	Video 6.1: The Story of Mount St. Helens Video 6.2: Oozy or Explody? Video graphic organizers (to accompany each video) OR Textbook Sections 6.1–6.2		Interview: Microconversations
6.3–6.6	How do volcanoes form, and how can they be classified?	Video 6.3: Anatomy of a Volcano Video 6.4: Shield Volcanoes Video 6.5: Composite Volcanoes Video 6.6: Cinder Cone Volcanoes Video graphic organizers (to accompany each video) OR Textbook Sections 6.3–6.6		Interview: Microconversations
6.7	What determines whether volcanoes are deadly or not? Can volcanoes have a global effect on the Earth?	Video 6.7: Volcanic Hazards Video graphic organizer OR Textbook Section 6.7		Interview: Microconversations
6.8	How is the global distribution of volcanoes related to plate tectonics?	Video 6.8: Plate Tectonics and Volcanoes Video graphic organizer OR Textbook Section 6.8		Interview: Microconversations

9

Creating Group-Space Learning Objects

Once you have developed, or at least planned, your independent-space learning objects, it's time to design or decide on the activities you want students to do during the group space.

I hesitate to go into too much detail about what would be an appropriate learning activity for the group space because what each of you teaches is so varied. Some of you who work with elementary students teach multiple subjects. Others teach advanced calculus or how to play the guitar.

What's most important is remembering that the filter is Bloom's taxonomy. In the group space, you will want activities to be in the middle (applying and analyzing) or in the top (evaluating and creating) of the taxonomy.

Group Work in the Classroom

Let's look at a number of excellent group-space activities that might pique your interest.

- **Practice.** As a physics and chemistry teacher, I find that much of my group-space time is devoted to students practicing physics and chemistry problems.
- **Questions.** Asking students a few well-chosen and targeted questions will get them to go deeper in a lesson.
- **Peer tutoring.** More able students can help out their peers if they wish to do so.
- **Debate.** Students can debate a controversial issue or an event in the past or present.

- **Discussion.** Lead a whole- or small-group discussion about a topic.
- **Projects.** Have students demonstrate mastery of a concept by creating a project.
- **Project-based learning.** You can use this approach in a multitude of lessons. I highly recommend picking up a copy of Dan Jones's book *Flipped 3.0 Project Based Learning: An Insanely Simple Guide* (2018).
- **Simulations.** Many online and offline simulations exist that can help students delve deeper into a topic.
- **Socratic seminar.** Do some research on Socratic seminars and use this fantastic method to help students see different perspectives and develop their reasoning skills.
- **Case studies.** Have students work on different case studies and solve problems or develop unique solutions. In the medical field, professors typically present a case and students have to determine the treatment protocol needed to help the patient.
- **Scenarios.** A scenario is a simplified version of a case study that teachers can use to enhance learning.
- **Hands-on activities.** Mastery classrooms make room for hands-on activities. For example, as a science teacher, I can now do approximately 50 percent more experiments in my mastery classroom than before. In addition to doing experiments, students could create a diorama, program a robot, or even fix a car.
- **Manipulatives.** Many teachers, especially in math classes, have used manipulatives such as tangrams, base 10 blocks, and fraction strips to great success.
- **Peer instruction.** This is more than just having students teach one another. Harvard physics professor Eric Mazur, author of *Peer Instruction: A User's Manual* (2014), used peer instruction to engage his students. In this method, students are presented with a question, then each student commits to an answer, then students assemble in a group where they reason out the question together. Then they re-answer the question. At this point, the teacher clears up any misconceptions that students may still have.
- **Inquiry.** Use the inquiry process to help students learn on their own. If you commit to the inquiry process, your students would work in the group space first; the independent-space activities would follow to clear up any misconceptions.

- **Role-play.** Have your students role-play a historical event, a trip to the store in a world language course, the predator-prey relationships in a science class, or even classroom management scenarios.
- **First-person narrative.** Have students take the role of a historical figure and write from that person's perspective. For example, one teacher had students write a letter to President Martin Van Buren from the perspective of a Cherokee teenager who was walking on the Trail of Tears.
- **Social media parodies.** One teacher I know has students create social media posts from different historical figures. For example, what would a Twitter discussion look like between Thomas Jefferson and John Adams?

This list is not exhaustive; the sky's the limit, really. The key is designing (or finding) quality group-space activities that meet and enhance each lesson's specific objectives.

Adding Group-Space Activities to Your Plan

Figure 9.1 (see p. 82) shows my lesson guide. Note that I have both a hands-on learning activity—an experiment that simulates how lava flows in a volcanic eruption—and a series of essential questions. Students really enjoy doing this lab. They play with dish soap and then design experiments that test how lava (the soap) flows differently when heat, slope, or other variables change.

Regardless of how you design your learning objects, it's crucial to think in terms of lower-order Bloom's taxonomy activities for the independent space (understanding and remembering) and higher-order Bloom's taxonomy activities for the group space (applying, analyzing, evaluating, and creating).

It's time to get out your mastery unit plan and add your group-space learning activities.

Figure 9.1 Jon's Volcano Unit with a Complete Set of Learning Objects

Lesson	Lesson Objective	Independent-Space Objects	Group-Space Objects	Formative Assessment Tools
6.1–6.2	What secrets lie beneath the volcano and provide clues to how it will erupt?	Video 6.1: The Story of Mount St. Helens Video 6.2: Oozy or Explody? Video graphic organizers (to accompany each video) OR Textbook Sections 6.1–6.2	Lava Flow Simulation Lab 6.1–6.2 Question Sheet	Interview: Microconversations
6.3–6.6	How do volcanoes form, and how can they be classified?	Video 6.3: Anatomy of a Volcano Video 6.4: Shield Volcanoes Video 6.5: Composite Volcanoes Video 6.6: Cinder Cone Volcanoes Video graphic organizers (to accompany each video) OR Textbook Sections 6.3–6.6	2x Virtual Reality Volcano Activities 6.3–6.6 Question Sheet	Interview: Microconversations
6.7	What determines whether volcanoes are deadly or not? Can volcanoes have a global effect on the Earth?	Video 6.7: Volcanic Hazards Video graphic organizer OR Textbook Section 6.7	Analysis of Mount St. Helens Destruction Lab 6.7 Question Sheet	Interview: Microconversations
6.8	How is the global distribution of volcanoes related to plate tectonics?	Video 6.8: Plate Tectonics and Volcanoes Video graphic organizer OR Textbook Section 6.8	Mapping Global Volcanism Activity 6.8 Question Sheet	Interview: Microconversations

10

Creating Reflection Opportunities

With apologies to Edmund Burke, whose words I am adapting freely, taking in new information without reflection is like eating without digestion. I realize that some of you may not habitually use reflection in your classes, but it's a powerful tool for promoting both cognition and connection.

Reflection as a Daily Habit

When students reflect on their learning, their academic performance can improve (Lew & Schmidt, 2011). Melinda Mestre, a chemistry teacher in Australia, has her students reflect at the end of each lesson by filling out a simple form that she monitors. In her form, she clearly states the success criteria and includes three basic questions: *How do you feel about today's lesson? Why? What action should you take?*

I do something similar in my classes. Each day after a lesson, students must reflect in a Google Document on two questions: *What is something interesting or confusing that I have learned today? What is the next step in my learning journey?* Only I can see these reflections, and I typically respond to each one. Here's a sample of the kinds of things my students say:

- "We learned about convection with the example of boiling hot water with beans inside. When we looked at the beans in the water up close, we saw that the beans, because of the convection, were moving in a circular motion. The heat beneath the beaker made the fluid and beans inside rise to the top of the beaker. The temperature there was cooler, so the fluid (and beans) dropped back down again. It's also the last part of the first unit, so we read in class today. I also worked a little bit on my project about geological sites."—Abby, grade 11 geology student

- "Today we got to see some of the different chemical reactions in action (color and precipitate). We also got to use chemicals for the first time. For the next class, I need to study more for the element quiz and watch the video on Perusall, as well as finish up the lab questions from the lab we did."—Adriana, grade 10 chemistry student
- "Today I worked on understanding the relationships between speed, displacement, and distance. I still need to finish up Level 2, but at least I am getting a little better at it. I do not have full mastery over the subject yet. I am trying my best though, and I will try to finish Level 2 as soon as I can. I have all of the videos complete at least."—Ryan, grade 11 physics student

Note that Ryan was signaling to me that he was struggling. I was able to use this reflection to give him some extra attention.

These reflections take little time. I set an alarm to go off five minutes before the end of class to remind us to start the reflective process. I found this especially helpful when teaching remotely; the reflections served as an exit slip for students to leave our shared Zoom room. They also gave me deep insight into what was going on in my students' lives. For example, one student shared some personal information that I was able to follow up on:

> During this time of the coronavirus, my family has not been directly affected by the disaster. However, my aunt's friend unfortunately passed away due to the coronavirus, and the situation seems surreal. In addition, for the homework load this week, I haven't experienced too much homework.—Lauren, grade 11 physics student

Good teaching, whether you're using mastery learning or not, always comes back to developing quality relationships with your students. I didn't get into teaching just to be a science nerd; I also wanted, and still want, to connect with and inspire the next generation. I bet this is true of you, too. And establishing a habit of five-minute reflections is one more way to do that.

Adding Reflection to the Lesson Plan

It's now your turn to add reflection to your lesson plan. Because I have students respond to the same two questions each day, I simply add this information to the bottom of my plan in the Reflection Plan space. Here's an example.

In a Google Document, students will reflect daily on the following two questions: (1) What is something interesting or confusing that I have learned today? (2) What is the next step in my learning journey?

Take out your mastery unit plan now and add how you will have students reflect on their learning.

11

Assessing Mastery

In Chapter 1, I shared the two main reasons why mastery learning struggled to take hold during the 1980s. The first was the difficulty of figuring out when to do direct instruction; the second was the challenge of managing multiple versions of a test with 30 students in a class. This chapter will help you deal with these issues in your classroom.

If you have been using backward design, you should already have developed your summative assessment earlier in the cycle. It might take the form of a more traditional test, or it might be a project or an authentic task. When I taught traditionally, all students took the same test at the same time. But with mastery learning, students take tests at different times. Creating, administering, and managing those assessments can be challenging.

Although some of the expert mastery teachers I spoke with allowed students only one opportunity to take a summative assessment, I favor offering multiple opportunities. If you're planning to do the same, read on. If not, I nevertheless encourage you to read this section, because these management tips apply to formative assessment as well.

Digital or Paper Assessments?

Should your summative assessments be digital or paper? Figure 11.1 shows some of the advantages and disadvantages of each.

When Aaron Sams and I first started implementing the flipped-mastery model, we had three paper versions of every test. Some students who struggled memorized each test version, or, in some cases, students took cell phone pictures of the test and then shared them with their peers. We were in a quandary. Should we give paper or digital summative assessments? We eventually settled on digital because we wanted students to get a unique test every time they attempted a summative assessment.

Figure 11.1 Advantages and Disadvantages of Digital and Paper Assessments

Format	Advantages	Disadvantages
Paper	• The tests are more or less secure. • These kinds of tests are familiar to students.	• It's harder to manage multiple versions of a test. • It's not possible if you don't have a robust learning management system.
Digital	• It's easy to generate multiple versions of a test. • Tests can include color images. • Tests are entirely or partially graded by software.	• It requires a robust learning management system. • Test security may be compromised. • It's harder to grade written work.

Your circumstances might be different. You may not have a robust learning management system. You may not have the time it takes to create an assessment suite of questions. If you're in your first year of mastery teaching, don't feel pressured to change the way you assess. This may be your project during your second or third year.

The experts I spoke with showed great diversity on this topic. Many use software tools to deliver summative assessments, whereas others are old-school and prefer paper-and-pencil tests. Math teachers Corey and Tim in Germany use paper-and-pencil tests for all their summative assessments. They tried a few online platforms but found that too many students found ways to share the exams with their peers. Having only paper assessments available in class has minimized this problem. Other teachers are doing some sort of hybrid between online and paper-and-pencil assessments.

Meeting the Challenge of "Unique" Tests

So how do you create a unique test for each student? In 2008, when we started the flipped-mastery model, we were using Moodle as our learning management system. We discovered it had the ability to administer tests, so we wondered if there was a way to solve the problem of managing multiple versions of a test. Was there a way to give unique tests to each student? One day, as I was reading posts on a Moodle forum, I stumbled on a solution to my dilemma. When I realized what I had found, I did a dance in my living room.

Although we were using Moodle at the time, other learning management systems have more or less the same capabilities. I currently use Brightspace, and it has some of the same features. So do Schoology, Canvas, and Blackboard, as well as stand-alone assessment tools like Quia (www.quia.com).

Let's walk through what a typical workflow might look like for you to create thousands of versions of an assessment:

1. Start with your clear objectives or essential questions.
2. Create a bank of questions for each objective. I typically write 8–10 questions for each objective.
3. Let the learning management system or web tool randomly select questions. This is where the magic happens. For example, if eight questions assess Objective 1, have the system randomly pick one question to assess that objective. In other words, any of those eight questions for assessing Objective 1 could appear on a given test. For Objective 2, you might have the system randomly choose 2 questions out of your bank of 12 to appear on a given test. Repeat until you have built your test.
4. Each student will get their own exam, and it will differ from other exams. Some will have the same questions, but the exams will be generated randomly.

This may or may not work for you because it requires student access to computers. When we started this in 2008, we had eight computers in each classroom. Because students were not taking the exams at the same time, that sufficed.

Of course, writing good, meaningful questions that assess an objective is hard. During my first year back in the classroom, I scoured the internet for quality questions and was able to create the structure of mastery assessments. I also spent time that first year familiarizing myself with my learning management system. Small things like how to use mathematical functions took a lot of extra time. But once I learned how to navigate the tool, the workflows got faster. That first year, my assessments were just adequate. During my second year, I expanded the question bank library and deleted poorly crafted questions. Although this takes some time, assessing in this manner is very effective.

Ensuring Test Security

One challenge with a digital assessment is that students are taking an exam while they're connected to the internet. Sadly, this creates more opportunities for students to be less than honest. Also, students are taking the assessments at different times, so it's harder to monitor them in a classroom. Let's look at some ways to step up test security.

Designate a space

I learned this strategy from instructional coach Cara Johnson, who has done extensive research on mastery learning. She designates a space in her classroom for assessments, literally taping off a space that is only for that purpose. When students enter that space, they can only bring testing materials with them. So, in my case, that means no cell phones allowed. In this space, students' computers are always facing into the classroom so the teacher can check their monitors. If the students have anything untoward on their screens, it calls for an instant integrity check.

Use passwords

I put each test behind a password that only I know. When students enter the testing space, they ask me for the password, and I type it in. *Pro tip:* Some students watch my fingers and try to guess the password; to get around this, I have misspelled all my passwords and use ones that would be quite hard for them to duplicate. *Another pro tip:* Because different students might be taking different tests at the same time, I add a unique picture to each test as a backdrop. That way I don't type in the password for Unit 1 into a Unit 2 test.

Offering Practice Tests

This year, I tried something new. Through Brightspace (my learning management system), I allowed students to take as many practice tests as they wanted before taking the actual test. Because there are thousands of different versions of each assessment, I released each practice test without a password. For any questions that were graded by the computer (e.g., multiple choice, ordering), the students received immediate feedback. For long-answer questions, students crafted their responses, which I graded shortly afterward.

This practice might make some of you uncomfortable because you don't want students to see the test ahead of time. But remember, there are literally thousands of versions of the test. If a student takes a test 20 times (some overachievers did this), then those students are spending a great deal of time working through all the possible questions. Through sheer repetition, they will definitely master the content.

Coming Full Circle: Back to Paper Tests

At the end of last year, my colleague Amy Lindsey and I chatted about test security in our mastery geology class. She had been talking with some of our students; a few were honest about how some students had been cheating. Unbeknownst to us, they had browser tabs open that we hadn't seen. This year, we will print out different versions of our tests on paper (this is easy to do with our learning management system) and have students take the tests in the designated assessment space.

How to Include Open-Ended Questions

Digital assessments are easy to manage if you only include questions that the software can easily grade. But a good assessment should offer more than just these types of questions. In my case, some of the questions I ask are mathematical. I want to know if students understand the process; that's more important to me than just checking to see whether their answer is correct. If they got the process more or less right but got the wrong answer, I like to award partial credit for their work shown.

In the case of an open-ended question, I ask the question, which my learning management system will not grade. For example, one of the possible questions in my geology class is this: *Why is it that the higher the gas content in magma, the greater the likelihood of an explosive eruption?* Students type in their response, and I grade it. With some questions, students answer outside the learning management system. Take this one, for example: *Sketch a river delta, and label all the parts. Do this on a separate piece of paper and bring it to your teacher to grade.* For questions that are more mathematical, students must show their work in an organized way and then bring it to me after completing the test.

So don't feel as though you're limited to questions that are easy to grade. There's a way to manage a wide variety of assessment questions, and you can determine for yourself whether the student has mastered the material.

Keeping Assessments Short

Before I implemented mastery learning, I made my summative assessments one period long. To be honest, I did that because I wanted a quiet day. But if students are taking summative assessments more frequently and at different times, there's no need for lengthy exams. I've realized that I can create a rigorous assessment that takes students less time, so now my summative assessments are 20 to 30 minutes long. Having shorter assessments frees up more class time for student learning and interaction. And if you have limited access to technology and use a set of class devices, shorter assessments free up your devices; one device can be used twice to complete an assessment in a given class period.

Grading Right Away

Because the vast majority of my class time is spent "roaming," one of my routine tasks is grading summative assessments. Although the learning management system's testing package will give students a score once they complete an assessment, the students know that to receive partial credit for work or a grade on open-ended questions—and I always include those—they need to have a summative check with me. As I look over their work, I use this time for remediation. If I see misconceptions and related error patterns, I go over those with the student. Sometimes I ask them to verbally expand on an answer that had insufficient information to see if they actually understood the concept. If they're able to provide the missing information, I add points to their grade.

These summative checks are a powerful learning tool for students. They know that the stakes are high, so they take the assessments seriously. Also, passing the summative assessment early becomes highly desirable, especially for those who aren't motivated to take the test multiple times and haven't demonstrated mastery, because the last thing a teenager wants to do is give up their lunch or their off period to come in and take a test in Mr. Bergmann's room.

It Pays to Plan Ahead

Managing assessments can be one of the most challenging things in a mastery classroom. The key is to have a plan and stick to it. No doubt as you start, you'll need to change your workflow or modify your assessments as new tools become available to you.

12

Providing Remediation and Feedback

I hate to admit it, but when I first started teaching, if some students didn't get it, I just moved on to the next unit. I left those students behind. But with mastery learning, there's an *expectation* that some students won't master the material on their first attempt. And there's a plan for those students. As we look at the mastery learning cycle, remediation is our last element, and it's perhaps the most important.

By the end of this chapter, you should be able to complete your mastery unit plan—and you should be ready to start teaching using mastery!

Remediation: Strategies That Work

Significant research exists on the remediation process, and all the literature points to one important warning: if students don't get something the first time around, reteaching the topic the same way you initially taught it usually won't work (see Bellert, 2015). Unfortunately, I've done this more times than I care to admit. I find myself telling students who didn't learn something the first time around to "just watch the video again." That rarely solves the problem.

Thomas Guskey (2010), a noted mastery learning researcher, says it this way:

> High-quality corrective instruction is not the same as "reteaching," which often consists simply of restating the original explanations louder and more slowly. Instead, mastery learning teachers use corrective instruction approaches that accommodate differences in students' learning styles, learning modalities, or types of intelligence. (p. 55)

Although there is some debate concerning using learning styles as a way to teach, the premise is that we need to find ways to reteach that differ from the way we initially taught that concept.

So how do you help students who didn't learn something on their first attempt? The good news is that remediation isn't rocket science. The suggestions that follow are fairly easy to implement.

Hold small-group problem sessions

This is my number-one strategy. As I roam about the classroom, I'm continually checking in with students and formatively assessing their progress. When I see students struggling with the same concept, I instantly create a group.

For example, I recently noticed four students in my chemistry class who had difficulty solving a stoichiometric problem. They were working in different peer groups, so I asked them to meet me over at a table I designated. I handed each of them a dry-erase marker to use on the table's whiteboard surface and then did a small-group tutorial on the topic. I had them start the problem to see where they were stuck. As I watched them work, I realized they weren't actually struggling with stoichiometry but with a misconception about writing out chemical reactions. So I launched into a new explanation of chemical reactions, this time using manipulatives instead of the more symbolic method I'd used in my video presentation.

At that point, I left them and helped other students. I did this on purpose because I wanted to see if they could solve the problem on their own. Then I went back to check on their progress. I found one small error and corrected it. I then asked the four students to work on another problem independently. The interesting thing is that, before these students worked together in a group, they weren't really friends. But their shared struggle brought them together, and now they not only work together in class but also have become friends.

I used to have an interactive whiteboard in my class that served as a collaborative workstation for students. However, I didn't put it at the front of my room; instead, I put it on the side, so students could work together using online tools. This was especially useful in my geology class, where images, maps, and a search engine really helped students understand.

Maybe someday all classrooms will have interactive whiteboard tables to promote this kind of collaboration, but if your students all have tablets or other mobile devices, they can still collaborate in real time on digital whiteboards such as Google's Jamboard (https://jamboard.google.com). I found this practice especially useful when teaching remotely. For in-person teaching, I'd rather just use old-school whiteboards that students write on with markers; the analog system allows for a more tactile experience. I have even transformed my black lab tables into writing surfaces with the help of chalk markers. When taking summative assessments, several students routinely write on tables and then call me over to review their work.

Another benefit of small-group problem sessions is that they allow for better time management. If I can help four students at the same time, I don't need to work with them individually, and that frees me to work with *other* students. This is especially important if you have large classes, where it's difficult to tutor every student individually.

Offer individual tutoring

Probably the best way to remediate is through individual tutoring (Block, 1971). But this is sometimes hard to do if you have 30 students or more in your classes. Nevertheless, the fact is that some of my students need me to work individually with them during class.

I encourage you to be proactive with individual tutoring. I don't wait for students to ask me questions. Instead, I'm nosy, and I'm continually looking over their shoulders. If I see them making mistakes or notice that misconceptions are brewing, I address these right away.

Ask students to tutor students

Another beauty of a mastery learning classroom is that students who are ahead of their peers can assist their classmates. What invariably happens in my classroom is that when a student learns something new but their friend struggles with it, they just jump in and help. And we all know that when you teach something to others, it solidifies learning. But there's another important insight here from the tutored student's point of view: the student acting as tutor will likely have a different way of teaching the concept, and their way may well be more student-friendly than my teacher approach to the topic. A caveat here: I wouldn't make this a requirement, because I don't want to pile extra work on students who get ahead. But if students are willing to help in this way, by all means, let them.

Another creative way of doing this is to have older students help younger students. When I was teaching at Woodland Park High School in Colorado, top students from my previous year's chemistry class could sign up to be my lab assistant in this year's class; as such, they would set up labs and help out the students as needed. When Aaron Sams and I started implementing flipped mastery, we realized that these students were an untapped resource. The strategy worked exceptionally well. We decided to recruit students with the express purpose of having them help out in the classroom. In those classrooms where we had a peer tutor, we saw great leaps in mastery. Just having one more person in the room to help makes a huge difference. This year, I recruited students in AP Chemistry to come into my on-level chemistry class to tutor students. When these students are in class, the dynamic changes and students gravitate to their advanced peers for help.

Provide alternative learning materials

Several corrective strategies provide alternative ways for students to learn the content. Here are some of them.

Helper Videos

During the height of the COVID-19 pandemic, I developed curricular materials to help teachers teach remotely. During that project, I interviewed experts in online learning, one of whom was Paul Hennessy, a math teacher from South Australia.

Paul described how he creates *helper videos* for his students. These are super-short videos that address specific problems students have in his class. He begins by looking at a given assignment and identifies which questions might be problematic. He then creates a video that talks students through how they might solve the problem. I like to think of it as the over-the-shoulder video. When I decided to create my own helper videos, I asked myself what I would say to a student who asked me for help on a given problem. Instead of seeing me give this information live, students can now view these videos whenever they need help.

In fact, just recently a student asked me for the helper videos for a unit on collisions. I had gotten busy and hadn't made them. Needless to say, I created them, and they're now available for students. My helper videos are between one and two minutes long; making a set of them for one set of problems typically takes me about 20 minutes. I know this is a significant time commitment, but the beauty is that once you complete the helper videos you can reuse them every year.

Here is my eight-step workflow for creating these videos:

1. Open your online whiteboard tool. I use Google Jamboard.
2. Open your screen recording software. I use Camtasia (https://techsmith.com).
3. Connect your pen tablet device to your computer. I use a Wacom Intuos tablet.
4. Record several videos one after the other.
5. Batch-render (choose several videos to be created all at once) the videos using Camtasia.
6. Upload your videos to Google Drive.
7. Publish your videos to Formative (https://formative.com).
8. Link the Formative videos to your learning management system. In my case, Brightspace (www.d2l.com) is my learning management system.

Figure 12.1 shows an example of what students see when they go to the helper videos. This particular video is on stoichiometry, which has to do with the quantitative relationship among constituents in a chemical substance. Notice that I've posted the actual problem set, with a helper video on the right. Students simply click on the video, and my explanation pops up. To watch one of my helper videos, go to https://bit.ly/helpervideo.

Videos That Others Have Created

Sometimes students don't learn as well from my videos as they do from another teacher's video. When we first started the flipped-learning journey, Aaron Sams and I created separate videos for our chemistry classes. The videos covered the same topics. One day, a student came up to me and said that he had learned better from Mr. Sams's videos. To be honest, that perturbed me at first. But then one of Aaron's students said the same thing about my videos. After I got over myself, I came to the conclusion that I don't care where students learn what they need to learn. I just care that they learn it, one way or the other. Our job is to ensure that students get a good education; I don't have to be the sole source of that learning.

Ashhurst Primary School in New Zealand does this particularly well. Teachers who teach the same level and topic create their own videos for the most part. But because the school has completely embraced mastery learning, they have a simple sharing system where teachers can easily find other Ashhurst-created videos. Teachers then share links to those videos with their students.

Figure 12.1 Helper Video Content

Worksheet 7.1 Stoichiometry

1. Carbon disulfide is an important industrial solvent. It is prepared by the reaction of coke with sulfur dioxide:

    $$5C(s) + 2SO_2(g) \longrightarrow CS_2 + 4CO(g)$$

    a. How many moles of CS_2 form when 6.3 mol of C reacts?

    b. How many moles of carbo are needed to react with 7.24 moles of SO_2?

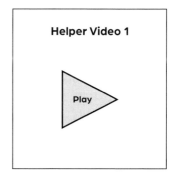

2. Silver can be made according to the following equation:

    $$\underline{\quad} AgNO_2 + \underline{\quad} Ca \rightarrow \underline{\quad} Ca(NO_2)_2 + \underline{\quad} Ag$$

    ☐ Balance the equation.
    ☐ If 35.3 moles of silver nitrate are reacted, how many moles of silver are produced?

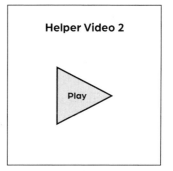

3. Ammonia is formed from this reaction:

    $$\underline{\quad} N_2 + \underline{\quad} H_2 \rightarrow \underline{\quad} NH_3$$

    ☐ Balance the equation.
    ☐ How many moles of ammonia are formed if 6.00 moles of hydrogen react with excess nitrogen gas?

4. Potassium chlorate decomposes according to the following reaction:

    $$\underline{\quad} KCl_3 \rightarrow \underline{\quad} KCl + \underline{\quad} O_2$$

    ☐ Balance the equation.
    ☐ How many moles of potassium chlorate are needed to produce 15.0 moles of oxygen gas?

A Range of Readings

Remember that independent-space work doesn't just have to be videos. It can be textual. Giving students a range of texts to read can be an effective corrective. I have often found that the readings I assign from the textbook are at too high of a reading level for my students, so I look for better explanations and have students who need extra help link to those readings. I have used https://physicsclassroom.com as a reading source for students to learn specific content. This site was created by physics teachers for both physics students and teachers. I encourage you to find similar sites and sources that teach your topic at the appropriate level.

Alternative Problems and Assignments

Having parallel problems and assignments for students who need extra help will assist students who struggle. I build these into my existing assignments. When creating a question set, I typically write double the number of questions I think are necessary. I scaffold the assignment from easier to harder, so the questions get progressively more difficult as you go along. Students know to do just the odd-number questions. When I find students struggling, I offer some on-the-spot remediation and then ask them to complete a few of the even-number exercises as well, just to confirm that they now understand how to do those problems correctly.

Games, Simulations, and Puzzles

Games, simulations, and puzzles can also be an effective way for students to get remediation. I have found great resources at Teachers Pay Teachers (www.teacherspayteachers.com) and at other online sources. As a science teacher, I have found simulations to be an especially powerful tool for learning. I am a fan of the PhET simulations from the University of Colorado (https://phet.colorado.edu), which enable students to do virtual experiments where they can alter variables and quickly see what happens. Just next week, we will be doing two electricity simulations that allow students to see how charge flows through an electrical circuit. When struggling students do simulations collaboratively, I have seen great results.

Your Remediation Plan

Finally, it's time to add the last piece of your mastery learning unit: the remediation plan. Unlike the previous planning decisions, rather than settle on one alternative approach or the other, you'll want to select several approaches; some correctives will work best for some students and other correctives for others. Most likely, small-group problem sessions and individual tutoring will always be a part of your remediation plan.

To go back inside my head for a moment, my plan for helping students who don't master the material on volcanoes will consist of three alternatives: small-group problem sessions, individual tutoring, and alternative texts.

Now it's time for you to complete your mastery unit plan. Add your remediation plan, and you should be done.

A Completed Mastery Unit Plan

Figure 12.2 shows my completed mastery unit plan for my volcano unit.

Figure 12.2 Completed Plan for Jon's Volcano Unit

Driving Question(s)

What are the types, causes, and effects of volcanic activity on the Earth?

Clear Unit Objectives/Essential Questions

- What secrets lie beneath the volcano and provide clues to how it will erupt? (Lessons 6.1–6.2)
- How do volcanoes form, and how can they be classified? (Lessons 6.3–6.6)
- What determines whether volcanoes are deadly or not? (Lesson 6.7)
- Can volcanoes have a global effect on the Earth? (Lesson 6.7)
- How is the global distribution of volcanoes related to plate tectonics? (Lesson 6.8)

Volcano Unit Mastery Rubric (Mission Tracker)

Lesson	Lesson Objective	Proof of Basic Understanding "I sort of get it."	Proof of Clear Understanding "I get it."	Proof of Deeper Understanding "I really get it."
6.1–6.2	What secrets lie beneath the volcano and provide clues to how it will erupt?	• Explain the causes of the Mount St. Helens eruption. AND • Explain how the viscosity of magma helps identify how the volcano will erupt.	• Compare and contrast the silica content, viscosity, and explosiveness of the different types of magma. AND • Infer the most important component of magma in determining the explosiveness of a volcanic eruption.	• Design an experiment that models the viscosity flow of a volcano and illustrates how it erupts. OR • Model the effect of trapped gases on the explosiveness of magma and the behavior of solid particles in magma using raisins, vinegar, and baking soda.

(continued)

Figure 12.2 Completed Plan for Jon's Volcano Unit—*(continued)*

Lesson	Lesson Objective	Proof of Basic Understanding "I sort of get it."	Proof of Clear Understanding "I get it."	Proof of Deeper Understanding "I really get it."
6.3–6.6	How do volcanoes form, and how can they be classified?	• Sketch the three main types of volcanoes and explain how each forms. AND • Explain how the type of volcano determines how it will erupt. AND • Give at least two examples of each of the three main types of volcanoes.	• Explain how the type of magma is related to the type of eruption that will occur. AND • Explain how the slope of a volcano is indicative of the type of igneous rock from which it was made.	• Connect Bowen's reaction series to the type of volcano formed. OR • Choose one volcano. Explain its unique geology and what caused it to form or erupt in the way that it did.
6.7	What determines whether volcanoes are deadly or not? Can volcanoes have a global effect on the Earth?	• List the eight types of hazards posed by volcanoes. AND • List at least four effects volcanoes have on the entire Earth. AND • Explain the Volcanic Explosivity Index (VEI), and contrast three different volcanic eruptions.	• Explain the eight different hazards of volcanoes. Select the one you believe is the most damaging. Support your choice with evidence. AND • Choose the hazard that you think is least damaging and support your ideas in a three- to four-paragraph essay.	• Write a first-person narrative of someone who lived through a major eruption. OR • Create a video that describes what you believe is the greatest threat that volcanoes pose to the world. Support your choice with evidence. OR • Write a short narrative of what it would be like if the Yellowstone supervolcano were to erupt.

Lesson	Lesson Objective	Proof of Basic Understanding "I sort of get it."	Proof of Clear Understanding "I get it."	Proof of Deeper Understanding "I really get it."
6.8	How is the global distribution of volcanoes related to plate tectonics?	• Sketch the ring of fire, and discuss how this relates to how some volcanoes form. AND • Identify global patterns of earthquake and volcanic activity.	• Contrast a hotspot volcano with a subduction zone volcano and explain their respective origins.	• Create a simulation that shows how a hotspot volcano can create a series of volcanoes over millions of years.

Summative Assessment Plan

- Students will choose to take one or more of three different summative assessments—for *basic, clear,* or *deeper* understanding. The highest level they pass determines their grade.
- Students must score a minimum of 80 percent on whichever test they choose.
- If students choose the deeper understanding assessment, they must complete a five-minute interview with me in which I check for true deeper understanding. The focus of that conversation will be the question *What are the types, causes, and effects of volcanic activity on the Earth?*

Pre-Test Plan

None needed for this unit.

Volcano Lesson Plan

Lesson	Lesson Objective	Independent-Space Objects	Group-Space Objects	Formative Assessment Tools
6.1–6.2	What secrets lie beneath the volcano and provide clues to how it will erupt?	Video 6.1: The Story of Mount St. Helens Video 6.2: Oozy or Explody? Video graphic organizers (to accompany each video) OR Textbook Sections 6.1–6.2	Lava Flow Simulation Lab 6.1–6.2 Question Sheet	Interview: Microconversations

(continued)

Lesson	Lesson Objective	Independent-Space Objects	Group-Space Objects	Formative Assessment Tools
6.3–6.6	How do volcanoes form, and how can they be classified?	Video 6.3: Anatomy of a Volcano Video 6.4: Shield Volcanoes Video 6.5: Composite Volcanoes Video 6.6: Cinder Cone Volcanoes Video graphic organizers (to accompany each video) OR Textbook Sections 6.3–6.6	2x Virtual Reality Volcano Activities 6.3–6.6 Question Sheet	Interview: Microconversations
6.7	What determines whether volcanoes are deadly or not? Can volcanoes have a global effect on the Earth?	Video 6.7: Volcanic Hazards Video graphic organizer OR Textbook Section 6.7	Analysis of Mount St. Helens Destruction Lab 6.7 Question Sheet	Interview: Microconversations
6.8	How is the global distribution of volcanoes related to plate tectonics?	Video 6.8: Plate Tectonics and Volcanoes Video graphic organizer OR Textbook Section 6.8	Mapping Global Volcanism Activity 6.8 Question Sheet	Interview: Microconversations

Remediation Plan

Supports for students who don't master the topic of volcanoes:
- Small-group problem sessions
- Individual tutoring
- Alternative texts

Mastery Learning in Practice

13

What Everyday Mastery Learning Looks Like

You have already come so far. Your room is set up. You have created all your assessments and learning objects. You have your remediation plan.

But what do you *do* every day, as a practitioner of mastery learning? This super-short chapter presents the big-picture view you need to gain confidence and get started. Figure 13.1 illustrates the sequence I follow in a typical day.

Figure 13.1 Daily Flow of a Lesson

Before Class

Preparation is key when starting a mastery classroom. Before class, you need to make sure that all activities are set up. For me, a science teacher, that usually means I need to have multiple experiments ready. One issue I face is that I teach three separate courses in the same room, so I need to be able to quickly swap out activities and experiments. I have found that organizing these experiments in large plastic tubs works best. I train my students to put everything back in the tubs when they're done so that when a different class comes in we can easily start on a different set of activities.

In addition, it's crucial to review where students are in the curriculum. Some may need to watch a video, others may need to do Activity 3, and still others might need to take a summative assessment. Looking over my paper spreadsheet of who has mastered what helps ensure I have the right things set up.

Getting Class Started: Triage

When medical professionals are confronted with an emergency, they must quickly assess who needs the most help and which case is most severe. They call this triage. To that end, the first five minutes are the most important five minutes in a mastery learning class because I have to get to my neediest students first.

My typical introduction might sound something like this:

> Remember that by the end of this week, everyone should have mastered through Objective 3.3. Lab 1 should take you about 30 minutes, and Lab 2 should take you about 45 minutes. You need to make sure you get this done by Friday. If you're taking a summative assessment, I will come around with the password right away. If you're doing Lab 1, you need to meet me at Station 1 in five minutes. If you're doing Lab 2, the instructions are clear, and you can start without me.

The key to effective triage time is to get students to start on their next "thing." This is especially important because, if each student had to wait for me to come around and direct them, we would waste a lot of valuable time.

After the introduction, I make a point of going around and briefly chatting with each student or group of students to make sure they're clear about what they should be doing during this class period. For my more self-directed students, I usually ask them what they're going to work on that day. For those students who need more direction, I am much more prescriptive. For example, if I have a student with attention deficit hyperactivity disorder (ADHD), I will usually visit that student first during the triage time to make crystal clear what they need to do. If I don't get these students started right away, when I get around to them 15 minutes later, they often haven't begun to work on anything.

Roving

I spend most of my class time roving around the room interacting with students. What happens during your roving varies with each student or group of students. But to give you an idea, you would be doing some or all of the following:

- Helping students with difficult concepts
- Giving instructions to small groups
- Conducting formative mastery checks
- Getting students started on a summative assessment
- Reviewing summative assessments
- Posing questions
- Listening to students and letting the learning process happen
- Challenging students to go deeper
- Remediating students who haven't achieved mastery
- Connecting with students on a personal level

For me, the magic of mastery learning happens as I roam. I'm truly not the sage on the stage. Instead, I function as my students' learning coach. This roving time is the reason I do what I do. It's why I put in the extra hours setting up my class for mastery. After more than 30 years in education, I find that there's nothing like spending time interacting with students and seeing them learn, grow, get curious, and thrive. If you'd like a glimpse of what this looks and feels like, I invite you to check out the short video of my classroom at https://youtu.be/VQSa8OHyaGY.

Reflection

Near the end of class, students drop what they're doing and take some time to reflect. My phone is set to beep with five minutes left in class. Students know that ringtone; they know announces that it's time to reflect on what they've learned and on their next steps in their mastery journey.

14

Managing Students Who Master Quickly

When Benjamin Bloom (1968) first started researching mastery learning, he acknowledged that the approach would take substantial time because of the need to remediate some students. He went on to answer the natural next question: *what should students who* don't *need remediation do while the ones who* do *need remediation are receiving it*? Bloom proposed teacher-created or curated enrichment activities. His flowchart looked something like what you see in Figure 14.1.

Figure 14.1 Mastery with Enrichment

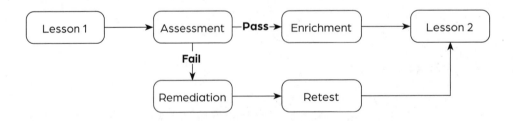

In the "I really get it" column of the mastery learning rubric, I have created advanced topics for students who pass the initial test. These students move on to the advanced topics while those who need more time continue to work at mastering the core objectives.

Of course, there are other ways, courtesy of the mastery learning experts, to challenge high-achieving students. Let's look at some of them now.

Declaring Minors and Majors: Hassan Wilson

Hassan, an 8th grade science teacher in New York City, has created a system in which students choose minors and majors. He designs learning cycles, and then his advanced students choose to do further study in their individual high-interest areas.

During the first semester, students must master several baseline topics; then, toward the end of the first semester, the more advanced students are asked to choose a minor. As you can see in Figure 14.2, there are six required areas of study and three options for a minor.

Figure 14.2 Hassan Wilson's Minors System (First Semester)

Required Cycles

Simple Inheritance	2 cycles
DNA Structure	1 cycle
DNA Fingerprinting	1 cycle
Protein Synthesis and Mutation	2 cycles
Genetic Disorder Project	1 cycle

Optional Cycles for the Advanced DNA Minor (choose one)

Cancer	1 cycle
Genetic Modification	1 cycle
Cloning	1 cycle

Note that the minor choices are a set of curated topics: cancer, genetic modification, and cloning. Hassan has created three different optional learning cycles from which students can choose. This obviously takes additional work; he's essentially creating more units of study than he would normally cover if he taught in a standard format.

During the second semester, Hassan ups the game and has all his students declare a major. The four majors are shown in Figure 14.3 (see p. 110).

Students choose their major about two months before the end of the school year. The number in parentheses shown in Figure 14.3 indicates the number of learning cycles in that topic. So, if a student chooses the Advanced Human Body major, they will do a cycle on body review, endocrine, nerves, and pig dissection. Because each cycle lasts up to two weeks, it takes about six weeks for a student to complete everything required for the major. Some cycles (marked with an asterisk) contain more complex challenges, and some (marked with a plus sign) require more advanced math skills. Hassan uses these codes to help students choose a major that is appropriate for both their abilities and their interests. Some students double-major or even triple-major. These students love to explore high-interest topics, and they learn as much as they can from his class.

Figure 14.3 Hassan Wilson's Majors System (Second Semester)

Choose a major from the following options and complete the associated required cycles.

Majors	Required Cycles			
Advanced Inheritance	Complex inheritance+ (1 cycle)	Sex-linked inheritance+ (1 cycle)	Pedigree+ (1 cycle)	Nature vs. nurture+ (1 cycle)
Advanced Evolution	Coevolution (1 cycle)	Human evolution (2 cycles)		Evidence of evolution (1 cycle)
Advanced Human Body	Body review (1 cycle)	Endocrine (1 cycle)	Nerves (1 cycle)	Pig dissection (1 cycle)
Advanced Evolutionary Genetics	Chi square and evolution+ (1 cycle)	Hardy-Weinberg equilibrium* (2 cycles)		Fitness and selection+ (1 cycle)

Hassan creates a workbook for each topic or unit. Then students work independently or in small groups as they master the material in the major or minor they pursue. Each cycle has expectations and benchmarks that students must meet to move on. Students must meet with Hassan for mastery checks so he can evaluate their progress.

As I ponder this model for my own classes, I realize that I would have to create almost one and a half years' worth of content to give students meaningful choices for their minors and majors. If you're just starting out with mastery learning, you may not want to develop this right away. Just getting a mastery learning program going is a large enough job.

The *A* Option: Bob Furlong

Science teacher Bob Furlong has a much simpler way to challenge advanced students. All students work through their learning cycles and must demonstrate competence in all topics. If they demonstrate competence, the highest grade they can earn is a *B*. If students want an *A,* they must choose the "*A* option."

For example, in a unit on biochemistry, the *A* option is to design a controlled experiment to show how a variable can affect enzyme activity. Students must design the experiment, get it approved, perform the experiment, and report their results. Students who complete this satisfactorily get their grade for that cycle bumped up by 10 percent. A sizable percentage of Bob's students choose this option.

The Grid Method: Hannah Curran and Holly Stuart

You can also organize mastery learning using the grid method developed by the Teach Better team (www.TeachBetter.com). Instead of using Bloom's taxonomy, teachers use Webb's Depth of Knowledge (DOK) framework to lay out activities. This is similar to the mastery rubric.

Let's look at two examples of grids developed by two expert teachers. Note that they start out with activities that are at the lower levels of cognition and escalate to higher levels, so read from the bottom up.

Figure 14.4 (see pp. 112–113) shows a math grid developed by 3rd grade teacher Hannah Curran. The grid shows four levels; Level 1 is at the "define and recall" level, whereas Level 4 is at the "inquiry and exploration" level. Each level has a stated *target,* the term Hannah uses to refer to her essential questions or clear objectives. For example, the target for Level 2 is "I can understand concepts of multiplication." Each level includes required activities to complete as well as assessment information. Note that Freckle is an online math assessment tool and Seesaw is a popular software tool for accessing digital content.

Figure 14.4 Hannah Curran's Multiplication Mastery Grid for 3rd Graders

Level 4: Inquiry and exploration **Target:** I CAN apply my understanding of multiplication to complex questions and problems.	**4A: LEGO Base Project** **Need:** LEGO Bases **Website:** Google Classroom **Assessment:** Project rubric and classroom presentation			
Level 3: Apply to real world **TARGET:** I CAN apply my understanding of multiplication to the real world through word problems and explorations.	**3A: Word problems** **Need:** Device **Website:** Student book pp. 44–45 H.5 Multiplication word problems	**3B: Seascape problem** **Need:** Device **Website:** Seesaw	**3C: Windows problem** **Need:** Device, Bridges Student Workbook **Activities:** Student book p. 55	**3B: ASSESSMENT**
Level 2: Apply and demonstrate **TARGET:** I CAN understand concepts of multiplication. I CAN show concrete and pictorial representations of multiplication.	**2A: Understanding "groups of"** **Need:** Device **Website:** Freckle **Multiplication Level 2, Tasks 1–3** E.1 Count equal groups E.2 Identify multiplication expressions for equal groups	**2B: Understanding repeated addition and skip counting** **Need:** Device **Website:** Freckle/YouTube Watch Video 1 Watch Video 2	**2C: Understanding arrays** **Need:** Device, paper/pencil **Website:** Seesaw/student book **Math Sheets:** Student book pp. 42–43 E.5 Identify multiplication expressions for arrays E.6 Write multiplication sentences for arrays	**2D: Level 2 MASTERY** **Need:** Device **Assessment:** E.9 Multiplication sentences

Level 2: Apply and demonstrate —(continued)	E.3 Write multiplication sentences for equal groups **Assessment:** On Seesaw, locate the Level 2A Grid Assessment. Using the microphone tool or video tool, explain what multiplication is in terms of "groups of" using equations and pictures. Email Mrs. Curran to have the assignment added to your Seesaw account.	Level 2B, Tasks 1–2 Student book p. 45 Student book p. 48 Frog Jump Multiplication Workplace **E.4 Relate addition and multiplication for equal groups** **E.8 Write multiplication sentences for number lines** **Assessment:** On Seesaw Assignment 2B, Grid Assessment, answer Question A using equations and pictures.	**E.7 Make arrays to model multiplication** **Assessment:** On our math grid Padlet, add a post that will explain what multiplication is using arrays. Use equations and pictures.	
Level 1: Define and recall **TARGET:** I CAN become more fluent with recalling multiplication facts.	**1A: Practice recalling facts** **Need:** Device **Website:** Freckle Multiplication Tasks 1–2	**1B: Practice recalling facts** **Need:** Device **Website:** www.timestables.com **Assessment:** Exit ticket on each level of facts	**1C: Loops and groups** **Need:** Device/digital workplace **Assessment:** Exit ticket or paper form of workplace record	**1D: Level 1 MASTERY** **Need:** Device **Assessment:** Freckle: Level 1 Assessment in backpack **G.1 Multiplication facts to 5x5**
Level 1: Define and recall **TARGET:** I CAN become more fluent with recalling multiplication facts.	**Multiplication Task:** Multiplication Level 1 Tasks 3–12 **Assessment:** Monitor progress on Freckle			**G.7 Multiplication facts to 10x10** **G.12 Multiplication facts to 12x12**

Figure 14.5 (see p. 114) shows a grid developed by middle school science teacher Holly Stuart. Again, start at the bottom and read up.

Figure 14.5 Holly Stuart's Science Mastery Grid for Middle School Students

Topic: Newton's Laws of Motion			Start Date _____	
Performance Indicator: Construct explanations for the relationship between the mass of an object and the concept of inertia (Newton's first law). Analyze and interpret data to support claims that for every force exerted on an object, there is an equal force exerted in the opposite direction (Newton's third law).				
Vocabulary: inertia, tendency, property, Newton's first law, law of inertia, Newton's third law, law of action/reaction, action force, reaction force, reciprocal				
Textbook Pages: Chapter 1 (Forces), Lesson 5 (Newton's Laws of Motion), pp. 30–37				
Level 5 Independent Exploration **Target** I can design a study to model the relationship between momentum and Newton's first law of motion.	5A Design a model.			Level 5 Mastery Answer one mastery question.
Level 4: Extended Thinking **Target** I can analyze multiple force pairs in real-world examples from my daily life.	4A Label multiple force pairs.	4B Model and analyze motion with multiple force pairs.		Level 4 Mastery Answer two mastery questions.
Level 3: Strategic Thinking I can explain how Newtons three laws apply to my everyday life.	3A Literacy Task: Directions and Article	3B Literacy Task: Graphic Organizer	3C Literacy Task: Three Paragraphs	
Level 2: Skill/Concept Target I can classify examples of motion as Newton's first, second, or third law of motion.	2A Quick Lab: What Changes Motion?	2B Quick Lab: Around and Around	2C Quick Lab: Newton's Second Law	2D What is Newton's third law?	Level 2 Mastery Answer three mastery questions.
Level 1: Recall **Target** I can define Newton's three laws of motion.	1A Highlight notes packet and complete illustrations.	1B Stomp Rockets	1C Vocabulary flashcards	1D Newton's Laws foldables	Level 1 Mastery Answer four mastery questions.

One exemplary aspect of Holly's system is that not all students begin at Level 1A. Holly starts each unit (cycle) with a pre-test and then places each student at the appropriate level on the grid. Some start at Level 1, and others start as high as Level 3. Her learning cycles are typically two to three weeks long. During the learning cycle, students are graded on their improvement as opposed to on how far they get. In the next chapter, we'll see how Holly translates improvement into a grade.

A Target to Shoot For

If adding enrichment activities feels too daunting to you, I certainly understand. I'm now in my third year of teaching after an eight-year stint out of the classroom; during my first two years, I didn't provide many enriching activities for my students at all. I was just too busy developing learning materials to make this happen.

The enrichment activities that we just looked at were developed by teachers after many years of teaching for mastery. Think of those activities as a target to shoot for once you have implemented mastery learning. The fact is, we can always improve. So put this on your to-do list for one or two years from now.

15

Grading for Mastery

I have a love/hate relationship with grading. Over my more than 30 years as an educator, I have moved from being a "traditional grader," assigning points and calculating percentages, to someone who believes in standards-based grading. I remember an occasion early in my career when I refused a student's request to round up a grade. This student had an average of 89.4 percent and was hoping I would forgive the .6 percent that separated them from an *A*. I told them that no, they hadn't earned the grade and that I was sorry. But honestly, was my grading system that precise? Did I really know they had learned exactly 89.4 percent of the material? No way!

When I started flipping my class, I began to interact more with students every day. I began to get a better idea of what was inside their heads and a better grasp of what they did and didn't know. Then, when I started using mastery learning, I truly began to question why I graded the way I did. Now I really *do* know what's inside my students' heads; I really *do* know what they do and don't know. And I now feel constrained by the traditional grading system I'm forced to work within. Most people think they understand what an *A* and an *F* represent. But do they really?

Later in this chapter, you'll hear from teachers who are working around the traditional grading system and creating ways to assess mastery. In the meantime, let's look at some schools that have adopted mastery learning and see how they've changed how they grade.

More than 10 years ago, Pilgrim School in Los Angeles, California, identified eight key values of their school, one of which is this: "Learners thrive in a safe and stimulating environment where the opportunity to grow from mistakes is valued." However, when they examined some of their practices, especially those with regard to grading, they realized that their system was actually penalizing student mistakes.. This led the school to completely redo how they grade. Teachers at Pilgrim still give letter grades, but these grades are linked to standards mastery. The school is moving toward a complete mastery transcript that shows specific targets that students have mastered (for an example, see https://mastery.org). When I talked with Patricia Russell, Pilgrim's chief learning officer, I was so impressed with the work the school had done to drive mastery learning forward by addressing the controversial issue of grading.

That all said, most of us—and that includes me—are working in school systems that grade traditionally. We can still modify our grading to better align with mastery learning. In examining how to do it, we'll look at three key issues: how to grade when you use formative assessment, how to grade summative assessments, and how to game the traditional system so it better meets your students' needs.

How to Grade with Formative Assessment

Natalie Victorov, a 4th grade teacher in Illinois, typically uses 10-question quizzes as the foundation for formative assessment. She expects students to score a minimum of 70 percent to demonstrate mastery. If some students fall short of that mark, Natalie provides remediation before asking them to retake a similar assessment; the vast majority of those students pass on the second attempt. If a student gets a really low score on the first attempt—for example, 20 percent—she flags that student for more targeted remediation.

High school science teacher Bob Furlong creates three formative assessment measures for each objective. He calls these *target practices* or "TPs." Like Natalie's students, Bob's students must score a minimum of 70 percent. A computerized system grades his target practices, and if students don't pass by their third attempt, the program flags Bob, at which point he intervenes with additional remediation. Bob notes that many students who haven't passed a TP after their second attempt actually approach him for help to avoid the extra remediation time.

Melinda Mestre, a science teacher in Australia, also expects students to pass all formative assessments with a minimum grade of 70 percent. But she has some wiggle room there. If she sees a pattern of misconceptions, she addresses those misconceptions and then expects the students to go back and redo the pertinent assignments or problems correctly. If they do, that counts as mastery.

Steve Crapnell, a math teacher in Australia, uses five-question quizzes as formative assessments. He expects students to score a minimum of 80 percent to pass (four correct out of five). Those who don't pass must do "correctives"—that is, after receiving some form of remediation, they must go back and redo the quiz questions. They also have to explain their reasoning for answering the way they do.

I'm a bit more relaxed with my formative assessment tools. Instead of settling on a specific percentage that students have to score, I use my professional judgment to determine whether a student has mastered an objective. This almost always takes place through a microconversation I have with the student. If they don't meet the standard of mastery for a given objective (as defined in my head), then they don't get credit for mastering it. I know this sounds fluid, but at this point in my career, I know when I see mastery—and I know when I don't.

You might ask whether the formative assessment grade should be part of a student's overall grade. Philosophically, I'm against this because I believe that *when* students master material should be irrelevant. That said, I do actually grade those assessments because I've found that adding a small number of points to the assessments encourages my students to take them. Shortly, we'll look at grading systems where you can determine how much weight you want to give to your formative assessments.

How to Grade Summative Assessments

The vast majority of the experts I interviewed stipulate a minimum percentage they expect students to attain on a summative assessment to move on. Bob Furlong only gives one summative assessment per learning cycle. His students can't retake that assessment, but they are expected to correct all their errors. Katie Lanier, a high school physics teacher in Texas, creates three different summative assessments. Students can take the exam up to three times, and they get to keep their highest score.

You might need to vary the minimum percentage you expect for mastery. For example, if you want an elementary student to master walking through a crosswalk safely, 80 percent just isn't sufficient. So you may need to adjust the level of mastery you require, depending on the unit of study.

That may well be ideal, but my experience tells me that my students need some consistent systems to follow. Because my high-achieving school follows traditional grading practices and all grades must have a percentage attached, I've chosen 80 percent as demonstrating mastery. I have found that this mark represents a reasonable level of mastery of my content. However, when I taught in a rural school with fewer numbers of high-achieving students, I made the passing mark 75 percent. Again, the number is somewhat arbitrary. But one thing is certain: when I share this system with my students' parents, they're thrilled. The conversation usually goes something like this:

> **Me:** To pass this class, your child must score at least 80 percent on every major assessment.
>
> **Parent:** That sounds great, but what if my child doesn't hit 80 percent?
>
> **Me:** Have you ever sat in a class and been lost? I mean *really* lost. What if I were to tell you that nobody in my class stays lost?
>
> **Parent:** So you're telling me that you're confident my child will actually learn the material and pass every assessment?
>
> **Me:** Yes. It's my job to be your child's chemistry coach. I get every student of mine to learn. I'll work with each of them until they master the material.
>
> **Parent:** But what if it takes them a while to learn? What if it takes them three tries at a test before they hit 80 percent? Will they be penalized?
>
> **Me:** No. Students shouldn't be penalized for learning material later than someone else. I don't care *when* they learn it. I care *that* they learn it.

These conversations almost always end with parents expressing gratitude. They realize I'm not out to get their kid and that I'm here to make sure they learn.

How to Game the Grading System

Teachers who grade for mastery have found ways around the traditional system to make mastery work in spite of their circumstances. Of course, mastery learning adds a level of complexity to traditional grading systems because students will be at different places in the content at different times. So how will you account for this? The best way to tackle this challenge is to look at some of the approaches that our mastery teachers have adopted.

When you can grade as you see fit

Unlike many of us, perhaps, science teacher Bob Furlong has complete freedom to grade as he sees fit. Nothing is dictated by either the state or his school. One of his courses has 10 units, with each unit consisting of between three and five lessons. Each lesson has several activities on which students are graded. For example, watching a video counts for 2 points, whereas his target practices (periodic quizzes covering three to four days of lesson content) are worth 10 points. Students must score a minimum of 7 out of 10 on every target practice. After mastering all the targets for a given unit, students take a summative assessment. In his system, students can only take the summative assessment once. He requires test corrections for students who don't score at least 70 percent; these are optional for those who do.

At the end of the unit, if students received a perfect score on all activities and target practices, they earn a 90 percent, the highest *B* on Bob's grading scale. This shows mastery. You may recall that Bob offers the *A* option, which enables students who want to go above and beyond to complete a more advanced task to show greater mastery. This extra work is worth 10 percent of their grade, and if they complete it to Bob's satisfaction, it will earn them an *A*.

Figure 15.1 shows a sample spreadsheet of one unit in Bob's course. Note that students must earn at least a 7 to move on in both daily assignments and the target practices. The bottom row on the spreadsheet indicates the number of possible points.

Figure 15.1 Keeping Track of the *A* Option: Bob Furlong

Name / Activity	1	2	3	4	TP 5.1	5	6	7	8	TP 5.2	9	10	11	TP 5.3	A Option	Corrections	UNIT 5 TEST	Total Points	AVG
Abbe, Andrew	2	2	10	10	9	2	10	2	7	8	2	2	10	7	19		72	174	82.5%
Banner, Bruce	2	2	10	10	7	2	10	2	9	7				0		14	44	119	56.4%
Gordan, Barbara	2	2	10	10	8	2	10	2	10	8	2	2	10	7	19	19	60	183	86.7%
Kent, Clark	2	2	10	10	10	2	10	2	10	9	2	2	10	10	19	8	84	202	95.7%
Lane, Lois	2	2	10	10	7	2	10	2	8					0		15	68	136	64.5%
Maximoff, Wanda	2	2	10	10	8	2	10	2	9	10	2	2	10	8			90	177	83.9%
Parker, Peter	2	2	10	10	9	2	10	2	10	7	2	2	10	8	19	14	44	163	77.3%
Prince, Diana	2	2	10	10	7	2	10	2						0			68	113	53.6%
Quill, Peter	2	2	10	10	8	2	10	2	7	9	2	2	10	7	19	17	66	185	87.7%
Rogers, Steve	2	2	10	10	8	2	10	2	9	8	2	2	10	9			72	158	74.9%
Romanoff, Natasha	2	2	10	10	9	2	10	2	10	7	2	2	10	8		18	64	168	79.6%
Stark, Tony	2	2	10	10	9	2	10	2	9	8	2	2	10	8			82	168	79.6%
Wayne, Bruce	2	2	10	10	9	2	10	2	10	7	2	2	10	7		29	42	156	73.9%
Points Possilbe	2	2	10	10	10	2	10	2	10	10	2	2	10	10	19		100	211	

When the grading system is predetermined

Melinda Mestre is a science and chemistry teacher in New South Wales, Australia. One big difference between United States and Australian schools is that the latter are preparing their students for a university entrance test that determines which university students will be able to attend. Students take this high-stakes test at the end of their final year, so much of schooling is geared to getting students prepared for that exam. The school where Melinda teaches uses both the state curriculum (New South Wales Education Authority), as well as the International Baccalaureate (IB) Middle Years Programme (for students ages 11–16) and Diploma Programme (for students ages 16–19).

The IB Middle Years Programme serves as a framework for assessing the state curriculum. Although I won't go into the details of the program's grading system, suffice it to say that it follows a 7-point scale. Subjects have four criteria—analyzing, organizing, producing text, and using language—that are assessed twice each year, and each criterion has a maximum achievement level of 8 points. If students get an 8 on each of the four criteria, they achieve a score of 32, which is then converted into the highest grade in the IB 7-point system—a 7.

In Melinda's classes, students complete a series of formative tasks over the course of the semester, which she grades in the same manner. If a student's score on the summative assessment is lower than the formative assessments would have predicted, Melinda has the option of adjusting the student's final grade. For example, if a student received a 6 on a Criterion A summative test, but she has evidence that the student is achieving at a 7, she can override their summative result and give them a 7 for this criterion.

Conditions differ when Melinda works with 11th and 12th graders. Because of the high-stakes test at the end of K–12 schooling, summative grades are almost impossible to overturn. Given that situation, she must give timely and accurate feedback to her students during the course of the year so there are no surprises for them on the high-stakes exam.

When summative assessments become the final grade

At Steve Crapnell's high school in Brisbane, Australia, up to Year 10 (14- and 15-year-olds), a student's overall grade is determined by three exams each year that are based on a curriculum designed by the Australian Curriculum and Reporting Authority. Students have one opportunity to take these exams, and they're taken on specific dates.

During the course of the term, all other grades are considered formative assessments. Because the students know that their total grade will be determined by the high-stakes assessments, they're motivated to do well on the formative assessment activities because these serve as excellent preparation for those tests. Steve keeps track of student progress in a traditional manner by posting student scores on all the formative assessments inside the student information system. Figure 15.2 displays the scores of one student, Alexandra, which both she and her teacher can see.

Figure 15.2 Sample Student Grade Report: Steve Crapnell

Alexandra

Due date	Assignment	Status	Feedback	Points
Yesterday	Prac Test 2 TF	Returned		1/1
Yesterday	Prac Test 2 TA	Returned		1/1
Jun 13	M6.3 The Parabola	Returned		5/5
Jun 8	M5.3 Quadratic Form	Returned		5/5
Jun 6	Prac Test 1 TF	Returned		1/1
Jun 6	Prac Test 1 TA	Returned		1/1
May 30	Quiz 5 Solve Quadratics	Returned		8/10
May 30	M5.2 Null Factor	Returned		5/5
May 25	M5.1 Nonmonic quad...	Returned		3/5
May 24	Quiz 4 Null Factor Law	Returned		10/10
May 23	M4.3 Surds Simplifying	Returned		5/5
May 23	M4.2 Surds Operati...	Returned		4/5
May 20	Quiz 3 Nonmonic qua...	Returned		10/10
May 20	M4.2 Surds (operations)	Returned		4/5
May 13	FL 22 Nonmonic qu	Returned		1/1
May 12	Quiz 11 Surds	Returned		10/10

Steve still allows students to go back and correct work they haven't mastered, as would be typical of any mastery classroom. But he is ultimately preparing his students for the large external summative assessment. His students have done exceptionally well on these assessments, and he attributes much of this to the mastery model.

A hybrid system: My "Version 1"

At my school, we're locked into a percentage grading system, so regardless of how I grade, I have to eventually give each student a number. The system shown in Figure 15.3 (see p. 124) represents how I graded for my first seven years as a mastery teacher. I consider this version a hybrid of traditional and standards-based grading. Later, I will share a second version that shows how I have evolved into a more standards-based model. One of my limitations is that our science department dictates that we grade using a weighted grading system. Major assessments count for 50 percent, labs for 30 percent, and daily work for 20 percent.

In terms of daily work—that 20 percent of students' grades—I hand out unit packets that students work through to demonstrate mastery. The units are composed of separate quests that usually contain a pre-learning video or text plus a written set of problems or questions. The packets also contain all applicable activities, usually experiments to do, in my science classes. Each week, I inform the class which quests they need to complete by the end of the week. I check off each quest using a simple clipboard; students get either a checkmark that earns them eight points or an empty box, the equivalent of a zero. At the end of the week, I add up all the quests the students have completed and give them a cumulative grade for all quests they have mastered since the beginning of the marking period. The spreadsheet determines the student's weekly grade, and this is their cumulative grade, which you can see in the first column of Figure 15.3.

Some students will look like "Harrison Ford," who skips quests. Others, like our "Abraham Lincoln," will be a few quests behind. "Marie Curie" also fits that profile. By the end of the following week, additional quests will be required. If, for example, Marie Curie completes those new quests in order to get 100 percent for the week, she will also have to demonstrate mastery on the quests she missed from the previous week.

Remember, this spreadsheet represents 20 percent of my students' overall grade. Labs, which count for 30 percent, I grade traditionally, on a 10-point scale. However, I ask students who score below 80 percent on labs to redo them until they reach that (mastery) mark.

Figure 15.3 Sample Class Grade Report: Jon's Hybrid "Version 1"

Name	Weekly Grade Quarter 2	2.8	2.9	3.1	3.2	3.3	3.4	3.5	3.6	3.7	4.1	4.2	4.3	4.4	4.5
Total Points	112	8	8	8	8	8	8	8	8	8	8	8	8	8	8
Abraham Lincoln	79%	8	8	8	8	8	8	8	8	8	8	8	0	0	0
Sam Houston	100%	8	8	8	8	8	8	8	8	8	8	8	8	8	8
Maya Angelou	100%	8	8	8	8	8	8	8	8	8	8	8	8	8	8
Arthur Ashe	79%	8	8	8	8	8	8	8	8	8	8	8	0	0	0
Cate Blanchett	86%	8	8	8	8	8	8	8	8	8	8	8	8	0	0
Cesar Chavez	100%	8	8	8	8	8	8	8	8	8	8	8	8	8	8
Emilio Estevez	100%	8	8	8	8	8	8	8	8	8	8	8	8	8	8
Frida Kahlo	100%	8	8	8	8	8	8	8	8	8	8	8	8	8	8
Harrison Ford	64%	8	8	0	8	8	0	8	8	0	8	8	8	0	0
Lucille Ball	100%	8	8	8	8	8	8	8	8	8	8	8	8	8	8
Mahatma Gandhi	100%	8	8	8	8	8	8	8	8	8	8	8	8	8	8
Marie Curie	64%	8	8	8	8	8	8	8	8	8	0	0	0	0	0
Martin Luther King Jr.	100%	8	8	8	8	8	8	8	8	8	8	8	8	8	8
Mother Theresa	100%	8	8	8	8	8	8	8	8	8	8	8	8	8	8
Pope John Paul II	86%	8	8	8	8	8	8	8	8	8	8	8	8	0	0
Rupert Murdoch	100%	8	8	8	8	8	8	8	8	8	8	8	8	8	8
Steve Irwin	100%	8	8	8	8	8	8	8	8	8	8	8	8	8	8

As you recall, summative assessments represent 50 percent of the total grade. During a nine-week marking period, I typically have three major assessments that students must score a minimum of 80 percent on. If students fall behind, I'll temporarily put a zero in the gradebook. I do this even if they've made an attempt and scored less than 80 percent. This strongly motivates students to pass their summative assessments.

I then let the student information system work with all of the school-provided weightings, and *voilà!* Students get a grade.

Standards-based grading

Hassan Wilson, a lower and upper school science teacher, uses a standards-based grading system within a traditional school setting. At the end of each semester, he has to report a letter grade. The only grade that appears on the transcript is the end-of-year grade.

Each unit has content-specific learning targets in addition to the full-year targets, as well as specific science skills targets. All learning targets are tiered so students can demonstrate different levels of understanding, which align with the various levels of Bloom's taxonomy. Students can earn a Level 1 (remember/understand) through Level 4 (create/evaluate) on most learning targets. The teacher calculates the grade by adding up all of the levels a student has earned. For example, if being on pace for a marking period equates to satisfying a total of 10 learning targets, each with four possible levels, then the highest score a student can earn is 40/40 (10 learning targets, each met at Level 4). If a student achieves a Level 4 on 9 out of 10 learning targets ($9 \times 4 = 36$ points) and a Level 3 on the 10th learning target ($3 \times 1 = 3$ points), then the student earns 39/40, which is 97.5 percent, or an *A+* according to the school's scale.

At the beginning of a marking period, Hassan communicates which learning targets students need to complete and at which levels of proficiency. This is important to spell out because each quarter is not the same length, and some learning targets may require more time to finish than others. In addition, Hassan wants students to be able to calculate their grades on their own.

A few features about the school's reporting structures make this system easier to implement. First, only a student's final grade is reported on the transcript. This affords Hassan the opportunity to accept late and revised work. In fact, at the end of the year, students submit a portfolio in which they can include new evidence of having mastered a learning target that they did not master earlier on; if they provide this evidence, this results in an increase in their year-end grade. Similarly, Hassan can indicate a grade as incomplete for any marking period. This enables him to assign a deadline for students to submit new evidence that they have mastered a given learning target; if they do, he will change their grade from an incomplete to a letter grade. He prefers this system to one that might force him to incorporate zeros into the grade because zeros are notoriously difficult to overcome.

Andrew Swan uses his "I get it" rubric to give an *A*, *B*, or *C* grade. (He doesn't give *D*s or *F*s in his class because *C* equals "You sort of get it," *B* equals "You get it," and *A* equals "You totally get it.") Figure 15.4 shows how a student got three different grades on three different missions.

Figure 15.4 Sample Grading Rubric: Andrew Swan

What Is Government? Who Needs It?!

	YOUR MISSIONS	Proof of Basic Understanding "You sort of get it."	Proof of Clear Understanding "You get it!"	Proof of Deeper Understanding "You totally get it!"
C	1. I can explain why all communities have some form of government.	☑ List three ways that a government can help a community. AND ☑ Understand the meaning of these "Need-2Know terms": constitution, autocracy, republic, direct democracy, rule of law, and common good/welfare.	☐ Explain why all communities need some form of government *(include at least three "Need-2Know terms")*. AND ☑ Reflect on why your section's class constitution will or won't be successful *(provide at least two clear reasons)*.	☒ Reflect on why your section's class constitution will or won't be successful *(provide two clear reasons and include supporting details from at least one class activity and at least one historical example)*.

Grading for Mastery • 127

	YOUR MISSIONS	Proof of Basic Understanding "You sort of get it."	Proof of Clear Understanding "You get it!"	Proof of Deeper Understanding "You totally get it!"
B	2. I can analyze the concept of a social contract.	☑ Define "social contract" in your own words, with an original example from real life. AND ☑ Identify three different philosophers' ideas about the best form of government.	☑ Explain the major differences among three philosophers' ideas about natural rights and human nature. OR ☐ Create a dialogue among three characters that explains the major differences among three philosophical ideas about natural rights and human nature.	☐ Make a personal judgment about which is the best form of government or social contract. AND Provide at least two reasons why you think so *(include supporting details from at least one class activity and at least one historical example)*.
A	3. I can summarize the messages of the Declaration of Independence.	☑ List the topics of all five parts of the Declaration of Independence. AND ☑ Compare the Declaration's structure to another document.	☑ Make a "Handy Declaration" (https://tinyurl.com/HandyDeclaration) with original and appropriate labels for all parts. AND ☑ Reflect on the message of the Declaration's second part in the Mission 3 Reflection form at https://tinyurl.com/mission-threereflection.	☑ Write a Declaration of Independence with the same structure and messages as the original document from a different, assigned perspective (e.g., the perspective of John Hancock or Abigail Adams).

Let's unpack this figure. On Mission 1, the student showed evidence of understanding the two items listed under "You sort of get it," thus earning a *C*. The student skipped the item circled in the "You get it" column and received X for the item in the third column because they never did complete that item. On Mission 2, the student satisfactorily completed the two items in the "You get it" column, thus earning a *B*. On Mission 3, the student completed all items in all three columns, thus earning an *A*.

Eventually, Andrew averages the lesson grades to come up with an overall grade. This is the model I'm currently using in my classes— my Version 2. From a logistical standpoint, Andrew prints out rubrics for each student and fills them in as the student progresses. He also keeps track of their progress on a paper spreadsheet, where he leaves space for notes such as "Took four times to complete," or "Barely," or "Rocked it!"

As of the final writing of this book, I have been using this model for about six months. I'm pleased with how it has progressed. It works for both the students who master quickly and those who struggle. This year, more than any other year in my career, students are coming into my classes with significant gaps in their knowledge. I attribute this to the pandemic and to the learning loss so many are experiencing. Nevertheless, mastery has enabled me to meet each student's individual needs, something that would have been far more difficult with a more traditional approach.

Tying It All Together

Maybe you're like me in that you, too, have a love/hate relationship with grading. Maybe you're like me in that you believe one thing, but due to your circumstances, you have to practice something else. Regardless, I hope that you look at the scenarios above and find a way to create a system that will work in your context.

16

How to Stick with Mastery Learning and Not Give Up

As you may recall, my journey to mastery learning started when a transfer student, Gisella, came to my class late in the year and was nevertheless successful. But what I didn't tell you was that after one semester of mastery learning, I was about to give up. Because students were progressing at such a wide range of paces, running a mastery classroom seemed logistically untenable to me. I even went to my teaching partner, Aaron Sams, and told him that I didn't think I could keep doing this. But we stuck with it, and after some conversation and some trial and error, we solved the pacing issue.

But pacing won't be the only thing you're up against. This chapter will help you deal with the most common challenges you'll face when implementing mastery learning and overcome them so you can keep at it.

What to Do with Those Who Fall Behind

Let's start with the issue that almost caused me to quit mastery learning. During that first year, we found that most students kept up. But toward the end of the first semester, one group of students was clearly not going to finish mastering all the content.

In our curriculum, this posed a significant problem. The straggling group of students had mastered only about 80 percent of the material. But mastering subsequent topics—those they would tackle in the second semester—depended on their understanding the content offered at the end of first semester, so those students had to complete that first semester's work before they could move on. As you can well imagine, they just got further and further behind.

So how do you solve this problem? How do you deal with students at vastly different places in your curriculum? As a science teacher, I can't have 10 different labs set up at the same time. Logistically, I needed a way to manage a smaller range of things.

The answer turned out to be much easier than you might think. Aaron asked us to look at our curriculum and make some judgment calls about what topics were essential and what ones were not. In our case, the last unit in our first semester ("Stoichiometry") was the most important one in the entire chemistry course. In light of that, we rearranged the order of the units so the last unit in the first semester was *not* essential—that is, a student who missed the last unit could nevertheless be successful for the rest of the year. That most crucial unit from the end of first semester became the first unit in the second semester.

We clearly delineated between what I will call essential objectives and "nice to know" objectives. And because I have helped teachers in just about every subject move to mastery learning, I have found that there are always both kinds. So look at each of your units, determine which objectives are "nice to know," and put those at the end of the unit. If some students miss some of the "nice to knows," it's no big deal.

Most of the experts I spoke with have dealt with students who fall behind in a similar manner. Gilbert Ng, an economics professor in Singapore, says that he "strips down his tasks" into important and unimportant tasks. Alex Valencic, a curriculum specialist in Illinois, asks his teachers to identify power standards and to ensure that all students, at a minimum, master those standards.

As a teacher who teaches real kids every day and who wants to make mastery learning happen, my goal is for my students to by and large be on the same page during roughly the same time period. This approach I've adopted—being OK with the fact that some students haven't mastered the "nice to know" objectives—helps me do just that.

This solution may have some of you in a quandary. You may feel that you're doing a disservice to those students who don't learn everything you teach. This bothers me, too. But for what it's worth, I would rather my struggling students master 80 percent of the objectives than learn far less than that because they're expected to master—and then stumble trying to learn—100 percent of the objectives. I remember the days when I covered everything and some students got left behind. I now know exactly what my struggling students know and what they have mastered.

Why Students Fall Behind

This issue of students falling behind is arguably the biggest issue in all of mastery learning. I have found that stragglers straggle for two reasons:

- They're genuinely struggling with the curriculum and need extra support.
- They're not motivated to work hard.

I have much empathy for the first group. I'll spend more one-on-one time with them and modify their assignments. I also may have them skip some of the nonessential topics. I decide this on the fly as I work with the students.

For the second group, I simply do good teacher stuff. I communicate with the students about their having fallen behind, I connect with other adults in the school who might assist, I call their parents, or I work to find out what motivates them. The best motivational technique is for students to feel cared for and supported. Students who struggle will work much harder for a teacher who is invested in them.

Sometimes, like me, you stick your foot in your mouth and misclassify students. Just recently, I was working with a boy who had been consistently behind all year. I had classified him as a slacker; I saw he had great ability, but he didn't seem interested in doing anything with it. Then I learned that his parents were divorcing and that he was taking care of his younger sibling. "Basically, I'm like his dad," he told me. This student is also on our school's football team, which he sees as a way to escape the craziness of his life. Chemistry homework was not high on his priority list.

When I understood his predicament, I started finding ways to help him during class to lessen the outside-of-class burden. Wiser now, I'm resolved to see each student who struggles in a new light and try to understand *why* they're struggling. Often, it has nothing to do with the content or the student's ability. Often, outside forces invade the learning space.

What to Do with Those Who Get Ahead

I have found that there are two categories of students who get ahead—those who I call the *box checkers* and those who learn quickly and well.

"Check" the box checkers

If there's a dark side to mastery learning, it's those students who are just trying to finish fast. They don't really understand the material, but they like checking boxes. These will probably be your most challenging students. Students who fit this description in my class are frustrated: they turn work in, I give it back to them to redo, and they're annoyed because they believe they've already done the work. True, they *did* do it, but they didn't do it well, and they certainly didn't master it.

It's sometimes tempting to let the box checkers get their boxes checked. But I don't check them. I insist that students clearly explain a topic or perform well. For example, a student who had come close to an 80 percent on a summative assessment (the minimum score I accept) wanted me to let him move on. "After all," he said, "I'm almost there." But I held the line. He needed more remediation, and I was confident he would demonstrate mastery. The more you hold the line, the more students realize that the goal of the class is *learning,* not box checking. Although I haven't been wildly successful at this in my classes, I do believe that many students start to shift their thinking as the school year progresses.

Challenge and "recruit" students who learn quickly

For those students who are genuinely ahead, ideally, you should design enrichment activities to challenge them and place them in your mastery rubric. But don't fret too much about these students. When I first started with mastery learning, I had a student who was brilliant. She was curious, stayed engaged, and kept asking me for more. I created mastery units as fast as I could, but I couldn't make them fast enough for her.

You know what I did? I didn't worry too much about it. I simply told her that I'd have more activities when I had them and that she could work on other things during class. And you know what she usually did? She helped her peers. It was a win-win situation all around.

The Pacing Problem: How Can You Cover Everything?

How do you pace your curriculum when students are (at least in theory) working at their own pace? Personally, I set weekly benchmarks that I clearly communicate to students. For example, I announce on Monday that by the end of the week, everyone must get through Objective 6.3. I then monitor students and push each one to master what they need to master.

When deciding on the pace I want students to keep, I simply use my previous years' planning calendars as my guide. Past experience tells me, for example, that students will have completed Unit 3 by October 1, so the weekly benchmarks reflect that pace. Remember that students who are behind can skip some of the nonessential objectives, which helps keep all my students on roughly the same page.

Reach out to students who need more direction

When I first started teaching with mastery learning, I had a student, Vince, who had a severe case of ADHD. Giving him lots of freedom on when and how he learned didn't work out so well at first. This is because when I started class and stipulated what students would need to do that day, my higher-achieving students were often the first to ask for help. So I went to those students first. Then, after about 15 minutes, I'd get to the Vinces of my class, and much to my chagrin, they usually hadn't done anything with their time.

So I flipped the script. I didn't go to those students who *asked* for help first. Instead, I went to the students who *needed* help first. I always know who's behind because I track their mastery on the mastery rubric. I meet with these students and ask them to tell me what they think they need to be doing during that class time. They often don't know, so I simply map out what they need to do that day. Also, knowing that students like Vince can be easily distracted when working with specific students in the class, I make sure I put them in spots in my classroom where they can be most successful.

Stay curious about motivation

One thing I've learned from my many years of teaching is that different students need different motivations to be successful. Some students really respond to encouragement, whereas others need more of a physical trainer approach; they need me to be firm and direct. I can still build relationships and trust when I'm firm, and I believe that those students who need more direction realize in the end that I act that way because I care.

The Challenge of Tracking Mastery

To be effective, you'll need a way to track student progress. The experts I interviewed for this book had a wide variety of ways for doing so. Some, like Nikki Conyers and Amie Blackwell, create custom Google Sheets. Others are old-school and use a clipboard and grid. There's no right or wrong way to do this; a lot will depend on your context, your familiarity with technology, and what your school provides.

I've tried many technology tools to track mastery, and this year I decided on a more hybrid approach. I print out a blank spreadsheet, and then as I roam the room, I check off students who master different objectives. With so many software tools, I was constantly searching for the box to check off, so I realized that for monitoring for mastery, paper and pen were just more efficient for me.

But I still use technology, and thus a hybrid system. Every Friday, I digitize the paper spreadsheet and enter a summary grade for students. Although this takes me about an hour, it gives me a clear picture of where every student is on their mastery journey and sets me up to know what needs to happen the next week for each student.

Who and When to Help

One of the issues you'll face as you start teaching for mastery is deciding who and when to help. At first, I waited for students to get into trouble and ask for help. What happened? Some students constantly wanted my attention and seemed unable to do anything without my direct involvement. Then more students started this same pattern. I soon found that I had a long line of students waiting to either get help or get something checked off. And while students were in the line, they were not working on mastery.

I had allowed students to become codependent. I was helping some of them too much. The fact is, allowing students to sit in the struggle of learning is what leads to real learning. This is no different than when you work out. You need to put stress on your body and push it past the point of being comfortable if you're going to show improvement in your fitness. But there is a balance. You don't push beyond what your body can handle.

Learning isn't any different. We need to let students appropriately struggle and not rescue them. Learning *who* to help and *when* to intercede is more an art than a science. As I get to know my students individually, this becomes easier, but every day this is one of my key struggles. Here are two approaches that can help.

Use the cup method

When it's time to intervene, how do you avoid wasted time and the dreaded line of students waiting for your help? Enter Cara Johnson, a teacher at Allen High School in Allen, Texas. Her ingenious solution was to have a series of three stacked cups at each student's workstation. If a student showed a green cup, it meant the student was good to go and didn't need help. If the student displayed a red cup, it meant they were stuck and needed immediate attention. If the student displayed a yellow cup, it meant they needed help but that it wasn't crucial. This enabled Cara to quickly survey her room and know where she should intervene.

Group students in a mastery check

You will recall that I often use microconversations as a formative check. But instead of these happening individually, I conduct them in a group of students during mastery checks. Because most students are learning things at roughly the same time, many will likely track together. Often during the triage time at the beginning of class, I will identify which students are ready to be checked off for specific objectives. If I have a group of students—ideally, three to four—who are ready to get checked off on the same objectives, I form an instant group and have a microconversation with them. Keeping the groups small enables me to interact with each student; if the group gets any bigger, some students can end up dominating the conversation.

This practice not only saves time but also is pedagogically sound. When a mastery check happens in a group context, students benefit from hearing their peers work through their learning. This creates camaraderie among students, and the conversations are rich. The first thing I have them do is ask me a question or make an interesting comment. (I recall a student who asked me if animals could possibly help geoscientists predict earthquakes. He had heard that some species tend to exhibit strange behavior right before an earthquake. I didn't know the answer, so we looked it up. There are indeed some scientists working on using animal behavior to predict earthquakes!) Next, I ask them key questions derived from the mastery trackers that get at the heart of what they should be learning. Mastery checks bring me great satisfaction. This is when I see students having their "aha" moments. It's where their curiosity shines through. And it's where I truly build relationships with them.

How to Not Drown in Paperwork

Have you ever dreamed of not having to take papers home to grade? Of course you have. As Aaron Sams and I were developing the flipped learning model, we realized that all the minutes we were *not* spending teaching from the front of the room could be devoted to interacting with students—checking on what they are doing, how well they're understanding, and how we and they might need to approach the material differently. In other words, in-the-moment formative assessment can replace a lot of paper-and-pencil work that needs to be taken home. It's not quite the dream of paper-free evenings and weekends, but it still saves huge swaths of time.

My students know that to get a learning objective checked off, they must come to me with evidence of mastery. This is when I "grade" their work. For example, a student will come to me with their notes, a worksheet, and a lab that all demonstrate they have mastered a particular objective (essential question). I look over their worksheet and ask them to explain, for example, how they did problem 3. If they give an adequate answer, I'm confident they've mastered that portion of the objective. I do the same with the experiment they show me. If they have not mastered the objective, I give them specific feedback on what they need to do to master it.

One advantage of this model is that students have to actually master the content. Before mastery learning, my typical workflow was to collect the same assignment from all the students at the same time. I would then grade it and assign points. On a 10-point assignment, some students would get 10 points, others 8, and others 4. Do you know what I used to do? I just entered all those points into the gradebook and kept teaching. But did the students who only earned four points really master the objective? No! Now, if a four-point paper is turned in during a mastery check, I simply tell the student to go back and fix it. If a misunderstanding or misconception is at the root of the problem, I give the student appropriate feedback so they'll be successful on their next trial.

One strategy that has helped with my more math-heavy classes (chemistry and physics) is having students do only half of each assignment. They choose to complete either the even- or odd-numbered questions. If I discover some gaps in learning during a mastery check with a student who has completed the even-numbered questions, after providing some remediation, I'll ask them to do a few of the odd-numbered questions. That gives them plenty of practice, which will help them master the content.

This method also works if you teach a course that is less process oriented. My geology course is more descriptive than my physics course. My mastery checks in geology involve more conversation around, for example, how and why a volcano erupts. These types of conversations could just as easily focus on different subject matter, such as the causes and effects of World War II on the global economy.

Significant research supports giving feedback on the spot. Kulik and Kulik (1988) conducted a meta-analysis of 53 studies on the efficacy of the timing of feedback and found immediate feedback to be more effective than delayed feedback. So, if you need to save time and want to follow best practices, stop taking papers home to grade and do your "grading" in class with students present. Just to be clear, I still grade some assignments, such as large projects or papers, outside class time. But even then, I try to give students rapid feedback so they can improve if necessary.

Dealing with Isolation? Try Team Teaching

If there's any way you can implement mastery learning with a colleague, it will be that much better. Math teachers Corey Sullivan and Tim Kelly team teach. Instead of having separate classes, they have joined their two classes together. On an average day, they have 50 students in a room. One of them is usually grading work and giving feedback on mastery checks, while the other is answering questions and roving around the room. In the case of two science teachers I know, one is in the lab room and the other is in a tutorial room.

Even if you can't coteach in the same room, teaming with another teacher who teaches the same subject has many benefits, including the following:

- **It lets you divide the workload.** Setting up a mastery classroom demands work, and having a partner or partners will help with lesson planning, video production, assessment creation, and activity sourcing.
- **It allows you to work in your areas of expertise.** Maybe one of you is better as a tutor, and the other is better at assessing students. Maybe one of you is better at creating videos, and the other is better at creating assessments.
- **Bouncing ideas off a colleague will make you a better teacher.** What invariably happens is that you will discuss best practices and best ways to teach a topic, which will improve your teaching.
- **Students see you both as "their teacher."** Some students will relate better to one teacher than to another. That said, if we see all students as *our* students instead of *my* students, all students will benefit.

The Best Ways to Get Organized

It's crucial to organize all your mastery materials into a clear path for students to follow. They need to be aware of what they need to master. But they also need a simple way to access all the learning objects that you have created or curated. There are a variety of ways to do this.

Organize online

The elementary teachers at Ashhurst Primary School use a mix of Google Sites and Google Slides to organize their content. They break down mastery learning into a series of tasks that students must complete. For example, on the math section page for Emma Parkinson's elementary students, she lists the day's objective ("Solve division problems by equal sharing in ones, twos, and fives") under the heading WALT, which stands for what We Are Learning Today. Emma embeds a helper video under the objective and provides links to labeled practice tasks.

One thing I really like about Ashhurst Primary School is that each teacher uses roughly the same organizational system. This makes it easier for students when they switch classes, and it simplifies staff development. Figure 16.1 shows one of their shared documents for their Level 1 and Level 2 Reading Strategies section. Note the learning intentions, the links to flipped videos made by different teachers, and the name of the teacher who created each video.

Figure 16.1 Schoolwide Sharing System Using Google Docs: Ashhurst Primary School

Reading Flips		
Learning Intention	**Video Link**	**Name**
Reread to gain meaning.	https://www.youtube.com/watch?v=bSanv2pARK8	Emma J.
Match 1:1 (say the words you see).	https://youtu.be/V_eH1MzdTTE	Emma J.
	https://youtu.be/nOJ_GGBCJWY	Angela M.
	https://youtu.be/hqNLYeFbDfE?hd=1	Jane F.
Make predictions.	https://youtu.be/6yPHMmTTS7g	Kate R.
Relate pictures to print (read the pictures).	https://youtu.be/Y6S-dLLcIbo	Angela M.
Understand concepts about print.	https://youtu.be/gpCxMB1xSE8	Megan W.

Take a hybrid approach

Chemistry and physics teacher Megan Pierce uses a hybrid system. Figure 16.2 shows how she organizes her content into her learning management system. Notice at the bottom how Megan posts the unit's learning targets so students can access all the necessary learning objects.

Figure 16.2 Organizing in a Hybrid Manner: Megan Pierce

S1: Week 5	**S2: Week 14**	
S1: Week 4		
S1: Week 3	Week 14, Assignment 4 – Specific Heat Prac…	Due Apr 16, 11:59 PM
S1: Week 2	Week 14, Assignment 3 – Specific Heat Prac…	Due Apr 15, 11:59 PM
S1: Week 1	Week 14, Assignment 2 – Calorimetry Gizmo	Due Apr 14, 11:59 PM
Emergency Lesson …	Week 14, Assignment 1 – Edpuzzle – Heat an…	Due Apr 13, 11:59 PM
Reference Materials	Unit 11 LEARNING TARGETS	Due Apr 14, 11:59 PM

But Megan doesn't just post things online. She has students keep a ChILL notebook (Chemistry Interactive Learning Log). Credit for the ChILL notebook idea goes to Lee Ferguson from Allen High School, Texas. Students create this scientific notebook following specific guidelines, attaching a mix of their work and prepared three-dimensional cut-outs to the pages. Megan also has students take notes in their notebooks on the videos they watch using the Cornell note-taking system, which she taught them at the beginning of the year. I used interactive notebooks many years ago. After talking with Megan, I have started doing so again and am pleased with how it helps my students stay organized.

Another thing I like about Megan's approach is that it follows some research that suggests that when students do work on paper instead of using digital resources, they learn better. Researchers (Mueller & Oppenheimer, 2014) at

Princeton University did a study on digital as opposed to handwritten notes. They concluded that handwritten notes were better. They wrote

> When people type their notes, they have this tendency to try to take verbatim notes and write down as much of the lecture as they can.... The students who were taking longhand notes in our studies were forced to be more selective—because you can't write as fast as you can type. And that extra processing of the material that they were doing benefited them. (p. 1166)

Regardless of how you organize your content, you need to develop a system that's workable for you and easy for students to understand. My guess is that if you taught during the pandemic, you have a good idea about how to organize digital resources.

"I Don't Learn from the Videos"

Several years ago, I had three students who were convinced that they couldn't learn from my videos. To be fair, they struggled in my chemistry class. So I made a deal with them. I told them that if they watched and took notes on the videos, I would complement that work by doing mini-lectures with them in class. That's just what I did, and the students were successful. Sometimes others would jump in if they struggled with the same topic. That is one of the beautiful things about mastery learning. Because I'm not tied to whole-group instruction, I'm free to meet the individual needs of each student.

What If Your Students Keep Failing?

When I first started with mastery learning, I noticed that students who struggled to pass the summative assessment would often start to feel demoralized. They thought the bar was too high. If this happens in your class, consider offering three different summative assessments where students can demonstrate basic, clear, or deep understanding. I don't see this as lowering my standards. The key is to set the bar at adequate, high, and higher levels and then make sure you give your students appropriate remediation.

If students continue to struggle with summative assessments, consider the quality of your feedback. For me, the mistake I initially made was to ask students to simply rewatch the video or reread the book section. As we've established, it is important to have different ways to teach the same objectives.

Rewarding Mastery

Celebrations are good. When students have reached a milestone, acknowledging that success goes a long way toward developing a culture of learning and collaboration. For example, in my class, whenever a student passes a summative assessment, I ring a gong. That's right, a gong. Because I grade the summative assessments right after the students complete them, they know right away that they've passed. Some students have even come in at lunch to take an assessment, and when they pass it, they ask me to ring the gong—even though we're the only ones in the room. There's just something silly about a gong that motivates them. Other teachers have more tangible rewards, like stickers. All students, even my 18-year-olds, love to know that they've done well.

Gamifying the Classroom

Economics professor Gilbert Ng has gamified his classroom. In fact, he doesn't like the term *mastery* and, instead, calls his class *gamified flipped learning*. He has found that many of the elements of a well-designed game are also elements of a well-designed mastery learning classroom. Students are given a challenging task where they might fail. They learn from failure until they level up. Sound familiar?

Many teachers have either gamified their classroom or, at least, brought in elements of gamification to increase student engagement and achievement. I have dabbled with this myself and want to get better at it. In a conversation with science teacher Nikki Conyers, she showed me her "leaderboard." The leaderboard is a simple spreadsheet she puts on her wall that tracks all student progress on the class objectives. I thought I'd give it a try, so I used a whiteboard with a series of magnets as markers to do the same. For anonymity's sake, each student had a unique symbol that represented them. I was blown away by how much that board meant to many of my students. After they mastered a task or an objective, they would ask me if they could move their marker.

I know many teachers who are using software such as Classcraft (www.classcraft.com) to gamify their classrooms. Although I won't go into gamification here, if it piques your interest, pick up either Matthew Farber's book *Gamify Your Classroom: A Field Guide to Game-Based Learning* (2014) or Michael Matera's book *Explore Like a Pirate: Gamification and Game-Inspired Course Design to Engage, Enrich, and Elevate Your Learners* (2015).

Getting Buy-in from Students

Mastery learning will be new for your students. Effectively explaining this new approach is crucial. I've seen this done well, and I've seen this done poorly. In the latter case, I've heard teachers say something like this: "I'm going to try out a new method and see if it works." In essence, you're telling your students that you're going to experiment on them and that you really don't know what you're doing. How you explain mastery learning makes all the difference.

For me, this starts on the first day of school. I don't go over the syllabus. Instead, I use that time to stir the students' imaginations and spark curiosity. I also make sure they can access the school's learning management system, as well as a video I created about mastery learning. They're tasked with watching that video when they get home from school. I reserve the second day for question-and-answer time about the video, which discusses why mastery learning is so good for them. I also discuss how the class will operate; I explain the mastery cycle, the mastery rubric, and how assessments work. Finally, students from last year's class chime in on how to be successful in a mastery class. Those older students aren't actually present in the classroom, so here is how I manage this. In May of each year, I ask students to give advice to the following year's students. I simply walk around with my smartphone and ask them to talk to their peers. I've found that students are much more apt to take advice from their peers than from me.

The number-one thing students ask about is those multiple attempts on summative assessments. This blows their mind. In every class, one student will ask, "Mr. Bergmann, you mean that if we fail a test, we can take it again?" "Yes," I reply, "what I care about is *that* you learn, not *when* you learn." At first, they don't believe me, but after the first summative assessment, they get into the groove. Students ask about grading procedures, some of the logistics—and then we're off to the races.

If you'd like to see some of my beginning-of-the-year videos, you can find them at TheMasteryLearningHandbook.com.

Getting Buy-in from Parents

It's also important to communicate effectively with parents about mastery learning. Just as I do for students, I create an introductory video for my parents. In the video, I explain why mastery learning is a better way. I ask if they have ever been in a class where the teacher was yakking from the front of the room and they were lost. I also ask if they have ever furiously taken notes and found that once they gave their attention back to the teacher, he or she had already moved on. I explain that this will never happen in my class, that their children will learn and be successful. I even show them a picture of Bloom's taxonomy and explain that the students will do the hard stuff in class and the easy stuff, the information transfer, in the independent space.

I make this video jargon-free and try to communicate to parents and guardians how this approach will benefit both their children and them. For example, they won't need to hire tutors or be forced to continually help their children with difficult topics. They all took algebra decades ago, I note, but they probably don't want to spend time relearning it to reteach it to their kids. I also share some research on mastery learning to underscore that the approach works and I'm not experimenting on their children.

I use this video as prework for our Back-to-School Night—that is, parents and guardians watch it beforehand. During the Back-to-School Night, I take the time to answer questions. If you'd like to view one of my parent videos, you can find them at TheMasteryLearningHandbook.com.

Getting Buy-in from Administrators

Getting buy-in from your administrators should not be a big issue—I hope. Every administrator with whom I have worked in my consulting practice has believed in evidence-based learning and understood that mastery learning is backed by sound research. It's hard to argue with wanting all students to master the curriculum. But the reality is that the "we have never done it this way before" mentality might be your administrators' default thinking. As with getting buy-in from students and parents, the key is to communicate effectively.

Think about it: what is your administrators' top concern? My guess is that they don't want to get a phone call from an angry parent who says that the teacher "isn't teaching anymore." So set up a meeting with your principal and explain the mastery learning system. Tell them why you're doing it and emphasize that this will benefit not only your students but also, ultimately, the school. Listen to their feedback and make some modifications if necessary. When Aaron Sams and I started flipped mastery learning, we would often sit in our principal's office and brainstorm. He really helped us think through some of the logistics, especially in the area of grading and assessment.

Even as I work on this book, I see I have an email from my principal about setting up a meeting with him. He knows I've been writing this book, and, in a recent email to him, I mentioned that I've identified a number of new things I want to do next year. I think this set off a few alarms, and he wants to sit down with me and hear about the changes. He is super-supportive; he simply wants to simply understand the changes so he can effectively communicate with parents if they have questions about the approach.

Getting More Help Along the Way

You might recall that Marika Toivola from Finland shared how one of her goals in mastery learning is to get each student to a point where they fail. She won't know their level of mastery until they reach a "breaking point." Although I have tried in this chapter to anticipate all the issues you might face with implementing mastery learning, there are undoubtedly other "breaking points" you might come across that I have not addressed. In anticipation of this eventuality, I have created a help forum on my website. Simply go to JonBergmann.com/community and sign up for the free community. There, you can interact with other mastery learning teachers and get the help of peers who are on the same journey.

Conclusion

You might have noticed that much of the research cited in this book was conducted in the 1970s and 1980s. Although mastery learning gained some traction back then, it eventually fell out of favor for a variety of reasons:

- The technology tools for time-shifting direct instruction were not available in schools.
- Randomized assessment technology was not available.
- It's more challenging to design, implement, and teach for mastery.

This book is a complete handbook on how to implement mastery learning. We have looked at how we can use technology to time-shift instruction and create assessments. But how do we deal with the reality that teaching with mastery learning is more challenging? To answer this question, let's look at the field of medicine for a moment.

Anesthesia and Antiseptics: A Metaphor for Change in Education

I want to tell you a story about two of the top problems in medicine during the latter part of the 1800s. I first heard about this from Harvard physics professor Eric Mazur. I subsequently researched the topic myself and have found it the perfect metaphor for the state of education in the 21st century.

The first problem was that surgery was excruciatingly painful. Doctors learned how to do surgery quickly because nurses were holding patients down as they writhed in agony on the operating table. In 1846, William Morton, a dentist, discovered that he could use a mixture of ether and some other gases to put his patients to sleep during tooth extractions. He approached Henry Jacob Bigelow, a Boston surgeon, with this discovery. On October 16, 1846, the two of them anesthetized James Venable for the removal of a cyst in his neck. They were able to take their time, and Venable slept through the whole procedure.

Morton and Bigelow realized they had stumbled on something revolutionary. Four weeks later, Bigelow published an article in the *Boston Medical and Surgical Journal* where he shared the results, although he didn't share the composition of the gas because he was applying for a patent. However, he did mention in the article that the gas had an odor of ether. That information was enough for other surgeons to go on, and within three months, surgeons in almost all the capitals of Europe had used anesthesia. Within seven years, anesthesia was standard practice across the globe.

At about the same time, there was another scourge that made surgery extremely risky: sepsis, an infection that occurs during surgery. It's painful and often fatal.

In the 1860s, Edinburgh surgeon Joseph Lister was looking at the work of Louis Pasteur, which showed that spoiling and fermentation were the result of micro-organisms. Lister surmised that sepsis was caused by micro-organisms infecting patients. He experimented with using carbolic acid to cleanse hands and wounds before surgery. The results were astounding: his patients incurred significantly lower rates of sepsis and death. In 1867, he reported his results in *The Lancet,* a prominent medical journal. You would think that Lister's discovery would spread as fast as the work of Bigelow and Morton did. But it didn't. It took *40 years* for antiseptics to become standard practice in surgical centers around the world. Why?

In a 2013 article in *The New Yorker*, Atul Gawande analyzed the speed at which anesthesia and antiseptics were adopted and noted some stark differences. Anesthesia produced instant results; instead of patients writhing in agony on the table, they slept. The change also improved conditions for surgeons: conducting surgery on a sleeping patient was much easier than on someone wide awake.

In the case of antiseptics, the surgeon did *not* see immediate results. Because infections typically occurred one to two weeks after surgery, the surgeon normally wasn't around to see the negative consequences of inaction. In addition, surgeons conducted surgeries one after the other; at that time, they considered it a badge of honor to have a bloody smock. It showed they had a busy practice. Cleaning instruments, wounds, and hands and putting on new surgical gowns between surgeries definitely made the life of a surgeon much harder.

Why do I tell you this story? Because there are two kinds of change: *fast change*, which produces immediate observable results, and *slow change*, in which the results take longer to show up.

Think of the changes that have taken place in education in the last 35 years. Early in my career, I recall teachers who would blame low test scores on students' laziness. Although that still happens, many teachers are now of the opinion that if their students didn't learn something, they need to find another way to help them learn. Or consider grading. We used to record grades in an actual gradebook; now we can't imagine entering grades in any other way than electronically.

Or how about when teachers like my college chemistry professor prided themselves on their low pass rates, "weeding out" students who just couldn't hack it? That kind of attitude is, for the most part, gone. And what about the importance of social-emotional learning? Schools all over the globe have realized that if we don't take care of the social and emotional needs of our students, then they just won't learn well. Or how about when we used to believe that school had to be conducted in person, with teachers and students all face-to-face? Well, the pandemic certainly changed that in the blink of an eye!

So what kind of change is mastery learning? Clearly, it's *slow change*. Teaching for mastery will not make your life easier right away. It will be a lot of work. You'll have to rethink and remake all of your units, lessons, and assessments. You'll need to teach for mastery for a minimum of one year before you get into any kind of a groove. You may even have lower test scores during that first year. So you won't see immediate results. It will require a long-term commitment. And long-term commitments are hard in a world where we like immediacy and think there are shortcuts to success.

Making the change from passive to active learning, from traditional to mastery learning, will take commitment and work. But with time, you will see the results. And once you do, you won't ever go back.

The Challenge

You will also have students who will resist mastery learning because they haven't ever learned this way before. A parent might pointedly ask you, "Why aren't you teaching?" A colleague might criticize you because you're doing something different. And you could get pushback from your administrators who don't understand what you're doing.

But I'm asking you to stick with it, because mastery learning works. Over the long term, you *will* see your scores rise. You *will* see students more engaged. You *will* connect more with your students. You *will* change many of their lives.

You *will* be more satisfied with teaching. You *will* rediscover your passion for teaching. You will be a professional, doing the best you can for each and every student each and every day.

Are you up for the challenge? Are you willing to be one of those first surgeons who thoroughly cleans their instruments for the sake of their patients? Are you ready to commit to mastery learning because it helps all students achieve and receive an excellent education?

I know this book asks a lot of you. As it turns out, it's asking a lot of me. As a result of speaking with the experts and researching this book, I now see that I have to redo vast parts of my mastery classes. I have to meet with my administrators to discuss how I will assess and grade differently. I have to go back and remake many of my videos because I didn't put in the essential questions. I also want to create new assessments based on the mastery rubric. And I need to justify this to our parent community. I need to do this because it's so immeasurably good for my students.

The time for mastery learning is now. You can implement it slowly. Start with one unit or one class and set yourself up for success. I tip my hat to you for embarking on this great and rewarding adventure. Now go and reach every student!

References

Ausubel, D. (1968). *Educational psychology: A cognitive view*. Holt, Rinehart and Winston.

Bellert, A. (2015). Effective re-teaching. *Australian Journal of Learning Difficulties, 20*(2), 163–183. https://doi.org/10.1080/19404158.2015.1089917

Bergmann, J. (2017). *Solving the homework problem by flipping the learning*. ASCD.

Bergmann, J., & Sams, A. (2012). *Flip your classroom: Reach every student in every class every day*. International Society for Technology in Education (ISTE) and ASCD.

Bielaczyc, K. (2013). Learning communities in classrooms: A reconceptualization of educational practice. In C. M. Reigeluth (Ed.), *Instructional design theories and models: A new paradigm of instructional theory* (Vol. 2, pp. 269–292). Routledge.

Block, J. H. (1971). Operating procedures for mastery learning. In J. H. Block (Ed.), *Mastery learning: Theory and practice* (pp. 64–76). Holt, Rinehart and Winston.

Bloom, B.S. (1968, May). *Learning for mastery. Evaluation Comment, 1*(2).

Bloom, B. S. (1984). The 2 sigma problem: The search for methods of group instruction as effective as one-to-one tutoring. *Educational Researcher, 13*(6), 4–16.

Carpenter, S. K., & Toftness, A. R. (2017). The effect of prequestions on learning from video presentations. *Journal of Applied Research in Memory and Cognition, 6*(1), 104–109. https://doi.org/10.1016/j.jarmac.2016.07.014

Covey, S. R. (2020). *The 7 habits of highly effective people: Powerful lessons in personal change* (30th anniversary ed.). Simon & Schuster.

Farber, M. (2014). *Gamify your classroom: A field guide to game-based learning*. Peter Lang.

Gawande, A. (2013, July 22). Slow ideas. *The New Yorker*. https://www.newyorker.com/magazine/2013/07/29/slow-ideas

Guskey, T. R. (2010, October). Lessons of mastery learning. *Educational Leadership, 68*(2), 52–57.

Ironsmith, M., & Eppler, M. A. (2007). Faculty forum: Mastery learning benefits low-aptitude students. *Teaching of Psychology, 34*(1), 28–31.

Jones, D. (2018). *Flipped 3.0 project based learning: An insanely simple guide*. FL Global Publishing.

Kulik, J. A., & Kulik, C. C. (1988). Timing of feedback and verbal learning. *Review of Educational Research, 58*(1), 79–97. https://doi.org/10.3102/00346543058001079

Kuswandi, D. (2019). Effect of a flipped mastery classroom strategy assisted by social media on learning outcomes of electrical engineering education students. *World Transactions on Engineering and Technology Education, 17*(2), 192–196.

Lew, M., & Schmidt, H. (2011). Self-reflection and academic performance: Is there a relationship? *Advances in Health Sciences Education: Theory and Practice, 16*(4), 529–545. http://doi:10.1007/s10459-011-9298-z

Leyton Soto, F. (1983). *The extent to which group instruction supplemented by mastery of initial cognitive prerequisites approximates the learning effectiveness of one-to-one tutorial methods*. [Unpublished doctoral dissertation, University of Chicago]. https://www.proquest.com/openview/8830333e410f2e266c832e2132d0569b/1ProQuest

Massachusetts Department of Education. (2018). *Massachusetts curriculum framework for history and social sciences*. https://www.doe.mass.edu/frameworks/hss/2018-12.pdf

Matera, M. (2015). *Explore like a pirate: Gamification and game-inspired course design to engage, enrich, and elevate your learners.* Dave Burgess Consulting.

Mayer, R. E. (2021). Cognitive theory of multimedia learning. In R. E. Mayer & L. Fiorella (Eds.), *The Cambridge handbook of multimedia learning* (pp. 57–72). Cambridge University Press. https://doi.org/10.1017/9781108894333.008.

Mazur, E. (2014). *Peer instruction: A user's manual.* Pearson.

McCourt, M. (2019). *Teaching for mastery.* John Catt Educational.

McTighe, J. (2020). *The fundamentals of Understanding by Design* (Quick Reference Guide). ASCD.

Mueller, P. A., & Oppenheimer, D. M. (2014). The pen is mightier than the keyboard: Advantages of longhand over laptop note taking. *Psychological Science, 25*(6), 1159–1168. https://doi.org/10.1177/0956797614524581

Polsani, P. R. (2003). Use and abuse of reusable learning objects. *Journal of Digital Information, 3*(4). https://www.researchgate.net/publication/215439566_Use_and_Abuse_of_Reusable_Learning_Objects

Scheiter, K. (2014). The learner control principle in multimedia learning. In R. E. Mayer (Ed.), *The Cambridge handbook of multimedia learning* (pp. 487–512). Cambridge University Press. https://doi.org/10.1017/CBO9781139547369.025

Sturgis, C., Patrick, S., & Pittenger, L. (2011). *It's not a matter of time: Highlights from the 2011 competency-based learning summit.* International Association for K–12 Online Learning (iNACOL).

Tarbuck, E. J., & Lutgens, F. K. (2018). *Earth science.* Pearson.

Toivola, M. (2020). *Flipped assessment: A leap towards assessment for learning.* Edita.

Vitanofa, A., & Anwar, K. (2018). The effect of flipped learning through graphic organizers toward writing skill at MAN 2 Gresik. *Journal of English Teaching, Literature, and Applied Linguistics, 1*(2), 37–49. https://doi.org/10.21462/ijefl.v5i2.283

Wiggins, G., & McTighe, J. (2005). *Understanding by Design* (2nd ed.). ASCD.

Index

The letter *f* following a page locator denotes a figure.

active learning setups, 26
administrators, getting buy-in from, 143–144
anesthesia and antiseptics, 145–146
The *A* option, 111, 120*f*
assessments. *See also* formative assessment; mastery checks; summative assessment
    digital versus paper, 86–87, 87*f*, 90
    grading, 91
    length best for, 91
    in multiple versions, 12
    open-ended questions in, 90
    planning for, 47
    practice tests, offering, 89–90
    pre-testing, 53–54, 55*f*
    rethinking, 17
    test security, ensuring, 89
    uniqueness in, creating, 12, 87–88

backward design, 21–22
bins, using, 27–28
Bloom's taxonomy of flipped learning, 20*f*, 21
box checkers, 131–132

celebration, 141
change, fast and slow, 145–147
classrooms, mastery-friendly
    active learning setups, 26
    bins in, 27–28
    characteristics of, 12–13
    flexibility in, 26
    gamifying, 141
    keeping students on task in, 28
    multiple levels in, 27
    sample room configurations, 28–32, 29*f*, 30*f*, 31*f*, 32*f*
    station setups with purpose, 25, 27
    student choice in, 26
    teachers role in, 13–14
    whiteboard spaces, 27

collaboration, student, 12
competency-based learning, 7–8
confusion reports, 69
corrective instruction, 92
COVID-19 pandemic, 1, 15
cup method, 134–135
curriculum
    pacing, 132–133
    Winnetka Plan, 8
cycles of mastery learning. *See* Mastery Learning Cycle

differentiation, 12
digital assessment, 86–87, 87*f*
direct instruction, 12

education, changes in, 147
enrichment, mastery with, 108, 108*f*
equity, 13
essential questions and essential tasks
    in setting clear objectives, 40, 41*f*
    in video content, 65

failure, reaching and celebrating, 52, 144
feedback, immediate, 12–13, 136–137
flipped learning
    Bloom's taxonomy of, 20*f*, 21
    defined, 20
    described, 2
    gamified, 141
    role in mastery learning, 19–21
flipped learning movement, 2
flipped-mastery learning, efficacy of, 9, 11
formative assessment
    crafting questions in, 59–60
    grading, 117–118
    mastery checks, 57–60
    technology tools enhancing, 60–61

games, 98
gamified flipped learning, 141

grading
    formative assessments, 117–118
    freedom in, 120
    in mastery checks, 136
    rethinking, 17
    standards-based, 116–117, 125–128
    summative assessments, 118–119, 121–123
    timing, 91
grading rubrics, 126–127*f*, 126–128
grading systems
    hybrid, 123–125, 124*f*
    predetermined, 121, 123
    weighted, 123
graphic organizers, 66, 67–68*f*, 68
grid method, 111, 112–114*f*, 115
group space, 21
group space activities, 79–81

helper videos, 95–96, 97*f*

implementation of mastery learning
    administrators, getting buy-in from, 143–144
    backward design in, 21–22
    the challenge, 147–148
    before class preparation, 105–106
    cyclical versus linear patterns in, 22–23, 24*f*
    flipped learning in, 19–21
    online resources, 144
    organization for, 138–140
    paperwork, 135–137
    parents, getting buy-in from, 142–143
    reasons for, 14–17
    reflection time, 107
    roving time, 107
    students getting buy-in from, 142
    team teaching for, 137
    triage time, 106
independent space, 21
instruction, corrective, 92
interview mastery checks, 57

laptops, touch-screen, 71
learning
    competency-based, 7–8
    contextual, 13
    personalized, 8
learning objects. *See also* text-based prework; video prework
    defined, 62
    group-space, 79–81, 82*f*
    independent-space, 62–63, 77, 78*f*

lesson planning, components of, 56*f*. *See also specific components*

mastery checks
    grading in, 136
    grouping students for help in, 135
    interview assessments, 57
    microconversations, 58–59
    one-half approach, 136
    online, 58
    paper assessments, 57
    student-led questioning, 58
    student-taught content, 57
    verbal assessments, 58–59
    whiteboard assessments, 58
mastery learning. *See also* implementation of mastery learning
    barriers to, 9, 145
    defined, 7
    efficacy of, 9–10, 10*f*, 11*f*
    history of, 8–9
    in practice, 105–107
    rewarding, 141
    student comments on, 15–16
    technology access and, 10
    tracking, 133–134
Mastery Learning Cycle
    described, 22–23
    elements of the, 24*f*, 35*f*
    overview, 35–36
mastery learning mindset, 16–18
mastery rubric, 42*f*, 43*f*, 44, 45–46*f*, 52
Mastery Rubric Template, 42*f*
Mastery Unit Plan completed, 99–102*f*
Mastery Unit Planning Template, 36, 37*f*
microconversation mastery checks, 58–59
minors and majors approach, 109–111, 109*f*, 110*f*
motivation, 133

note-taking, 139–140

objectives, setting clear
    driving questions in, 38–39
    essential questions and essential tasks in, 40, 41*f*
    standards for, 38–40, 39*f*
    in video content, 65
online mastery checks, 58
organization for implementation, 138–140

pace, 12
paper mastery checks, 57

paper tests, 87–88, 87f, 90
paperwork, 135–137
parents, getting buy-in from, 142–143
peer tutoring, 94–95
pen tablets, 71
pre-testing, 53–54, 55f
puzzles, 98

questions
    crafting for formative assessment, 59–60
    embedded, in video prework, 68
    essential, in setting clear objectives, 38–40, 41f
    open-ended, 90
    student-led in mastery checks, 58

reflection
    adding to the lesson plan, 84–85
    a daily habit of, 83–84
    in practice, 107
relationships, 12, 13, 14
remediation plan, 98
remediation strategies
    alternative learning materials, 95–98
    individual tutoring, 94
    peer tutoring, 94–95
    small-group problem sessions, 93–94
roving, 107
rubric, the mastery, 42f, 43f, 44, 45–46f, 52

simulations, 98
small-group problem sessions, 93–94
social justice, 13
social learning, 69
spaces of mastery. See classrooms, mastery-friendly
standards-based grading, 116–117, 125–128
student-led questioning mastery checks, 58
students
    codependent, 134
    failing, 140
    getting buy-in from, 142
    giving choices to in classroom setups, 26
    helping, who, when, and how of, 134–135
    keeping on task, 28
    meeting individual needs of, 140
    motivating, 133
    struggling, reaching, 14
    who fall behind, 129–131
    who get ahead, 131–132
    who need more direction, 133
students, challenging high-achieving
    A option for, 111

students, challenging high-achieving—(*continued*)
    enrichment activities, 108, 108f
    grid method, 111, 112–114f, 115
    to help others, 132
    methods for, 14
    minors and majors approach, 109–111, 109f, 110f
student-taught content mastery checks, 57
summative assessment
    backward design in, 48
    creating, 50–51
    designing for mastery, 49–50
    differentiating, 140
    digital versus paper, 86–87, 87f, 90
    expectations in, 13
    grading, 118–119, 121–123
    online resources, 50–51
    passing, 13, 50
    purpose of choosing, 48
    retaking, 51–52
    tying to the mastery rubric, 52
summative assessment plan, developing a, 53–54, 53f, 55f

teaching
    active, 13–14
    post-COVID world of, 1, 15
team teaching, 137
technology access, managing limited, 10
technology tools
    annotating videos, 71
    formative assessment, 60–61
test security, ensuring, 89
text-based prework
    advantages of, 74–75
    creating versus curating, 74
    text interaction tools for, 75–76, 76–77f
    using a range of readings, 97–98
    video prework versus, 63, 63f
text interaction tools, 75, 76–77f
time, using for mastery, 13
triage time, 106
tutoring
    efficacy of, 10–11, 11f
    for remediation, 94–95
"The 2 Sigma Problem" (Bloom), 10–11, 11f

verbal mastery checks, 58–59
video creation
    audio quality, importance in, 71
    being yourself for, 73
    partnering for, 72–73

video creation—(*continued*)
    pauses, inserting, 73, 74*f*
    speaking naturally, 73
video prework
    best practices for quality content, 65–70
    creating versus curating, 64–65
    interactivity in, 66–70, 67–68*f*
    length best for, 65
    textual prework versus, 63, 63*f*
    tracking viewing behaviors, 70, 70*f*
videos
    annotating, 71
    central access points for, 72

videos—(*continued*)
    controlling the pacing when viewing, 73
    created by others, using, 96
    helper, 95–96, 97*f*
    introductory, 142–143
    for parents, 142–143
    posting online, 71

whiteboard, annotating videos at a, 71
whiteboard mastery checks, 58
whiteboard spaces, 27
Winnetka Plan, 8–9

About the Author

**Jonathan (Jon) Bergmann** is one of the pioneers of the Flipped Classroom Movement. He has helped schools, universities, organizations, and governments all over the world introduce active and flipped learning into their contexts. He is a frequent keynote speaker who challenges and inspires audiences with stories and real-life examples from his classroom.

Jon has taught at urban, suburban, rural, and private schools. He spent 24 years as a classroom teacher in Colorado before becoming a technology facilitator in the Chicago suburbs. When *Flip Your Classroom* became an international bestseller, he traveled the world for eight years as a consultant helping schools and universities move from passive to active learning. In 2019, he returned to the classroom, and his advice on mastery learning implementation is informed and enhanced by his own efforts to meet the complexities and challenges of teaching. Both research and personal experience have taught him that students learn best when they are active participants and that they don't care what you, their teacher, knows until they know that you care. He tries every day to connect with his students.

Jon is the author or coauthor of 10 books that have been translated into 13 languages. In 2002, he received the Presidential Award for Excellence in Mathematics and Science Teaching, and in 2010, he was a semifinalist for Colorado Teacher of the Year. He serves on the advisory board for TED Education and teaches full-time science and assists with staff development at Houston Christian High School in Houston, Texas.

Find out more about Jon at JonBergmann.com and explore the resources related to this book at TheMasteryLearningHandbook.com.

Related ASCD Resources: Personalized, Flipped, and Mastery Learning

At the time of publication, the following resources were available (ASCD stock numbers in parentheses):

EdTech Essentials: The Top 10 Teachnology Strategies for All Learning Environments by Monica Burns (#121021)

Flipping the Learning (Quick Reference Guide) by Jonathan Bergmann (#QRG118053)

Flip Your Classroom: Reach Every Student in Every Classroom Every Day by Jonathan Bergmann and Aaron Sams (#112060)

How to Differentiate Instruction in Academically Diverse Classrooms, 3rd Edition by Carol Ann Tomlinson (#117032)

Learning Targets: Helping Students Aim for Understanding in Today's Lessons by Connie M. Moss and Susan M. Brookhart (#112002)

Personalizing Learning in Your Classroom by Allison Zmuda and Bena Kallick (#QRG118049)

So Each May Soar: The Principles and Practices of Learner-Centered Classrooms by Carol Ann Tomlinson (#118006)

Solving the Homework Problem by Flipping the Learning by Jonathan Bergmann (#117012)

Students at the Center: Personalized Learning with Habits of Mind by Bena Kallick and Allison Zmuda (#117015)

Tapping the Power of Personalized Learning: A Road Map for School Leaders by James Rickabaugh (#116016)

Tasks Before Apps: Designing Rigorous Learning in a Tech-Rich Classroom by Monica Burns (#118019)

For up-to-date information about ASCD resources, go to www.ascd.org. You can search the complete archives of *Educational Leadership* at www.ascd.org/el. To contact us, send an email to member@ascd.org or call 1-800-933-2723 or 703-578-9600.

WHOLE CHILD TENETS

1) HEALTHY
Each student enters school healthy and learns about and practices a healthy lifestyle.

2) SAFE
Each student learns in an environment that is physically and emotionally safe for students and adults.

3) ENGAGED
Each student is actively engaged in learning and is connected to the school and broader community.

4) SUPPORTED
Each student has access to personalized learning and is supported by qualified, caring adults.

5) CHALLENGED
Each student is challenged academically and prepared for success in college or further study and for employment and participation in a global environment.

The ASCD Whole Child approach is an effort to transition from a focus on narrowly defined academic achievement to one that promotes the long-term development and success of all children. Through this approach, ASCD supports educators, families, community members, and policymakers as they move from a vision about educating the whole child to sustainable, collaborative actions.

The Mastery Learning Handbook relates to the **engaged, supported,** and **challenged** tenets. For more about the ASCD Whole Child approach, visit **www.ascd.org/wholechild.**

Become an ASCD member today!
Go to www.ascd.org/joinascd
or call toll-free: 800-933-ASCD (2723)

DON'T MISS A SINGLE ISSUE OF ASCD'S AWARD-WINNING MAGAZINE.

ascd educational leadership

If you belong to a Professional Learning Community, you may be looking for a way to get your fellow educators' minds around a complex topic. Why not delve into a relevant theme issue of *Educational Leadership*, the journal written by educators for educators?

Subscribe now, or purchase back issues of ASCD's flagship publication at **www.ascd.org/el**. Discounts on bulk purchases are available.

To see more details about these and other popular issues of *Educational Leadership*, visit **www.ascd.org/el/all**.

2800 Shirlington Road
Suite 1001
Arlington, VA 22206 USA

www.ascd.org/learnmore